GOD'S AFFLICTING PROVIDENCE, AND OTHER WORKS
By Francis Roberts

COPYRIGHT INFORMATION

God's Afflicting Providence, and Other Works
By Francis Roberts

Introduced by C. Matthew McMahon

Edited by Therese B. McMahon
Transcribed by Beth Saathoff

Copyright © 2015 by Puritan Publications and A Puritan's Mind®

Some language and grammar has been updated from the original manuscript. Any change in wording or punctuation has not changed the intent or meaning of the original author(s), and has been made to aid the modern reader.

Published by Puritan Publications
A Ministry of A Puritan's Mind®
3971 Browntown Road
Crossville, TN 38572
www.puritanshop.com
www.apuritansmind.com
www.puritanpublications.com

All rights reserved. No part of this publication may be reproduced, stored in a retrieval system or transmitted in any form by any means, electronic, mechanical, photocopy, recording or otherwise, without the prior permission of the publisher, except as provided by USA copyright law.

This Print Edition, 2015
Electronic Edition, 2015
Manufactured in the United States of America

ISBN: 978-1-62663-134-2
eISBN: 978-1-62663-133-5

TABLE OF CONTENTS

GOD'S AFFLICTING PROVIDENCE, AND OTHER WORKS	1
COPYRIGHT INFORMATION	2
TABLE OF CONTENTS	3
THE WORK OF MR. ROBERTS by C.M. McMahon	4
INTRODUCTION TO THE PROVIDENCE OF GOD	9
THE SERMON: *The Checker-work of God's Providences Towards His Own People, Made up of Blacks and Whites*	20
INTRODUCTION TO A BROKEN SPIRIT, GOD'S SACRIFICES	72
THE SERMON: *A Broken Spirit, God's Sacrifices, or The Gratefulness of a Broken Spirit to God*	85
INTRODUCTION TO THE CHRISTIAN'S ADVANTAGE BOTH BY LIFE AND DEATH	145
THE SERMON: *A True Christian's Manifold Advantage in Christ, Both in Life and Death*	155

THE WORK OF MR. ROBERTS
By C. Matthew McMahon, Ph.D., Th.D.

My grandfather always told me that if I ever found any manuscripts of Francis Roberts, that I should *read* them. Interestingly, at the time, there were *no* published works by Roberts of any kind. Outside of the work of Puritan Publications, there is still no other works available. My grandfather, a minister for many years, was an avid book collector and had obtained thousands of rare reformed volumes, of which Mr. Roberts was one (and I was the blessed recipient of my grandfather's collection). He read Roberts' theological works, especially his work concerning covenant theology (which is outstandingly good). And so, with this first volume we begin translating and updating the works of Roberts in our own day. If only my grandfather was around to see it! Yet, it is better for him since he and Mr. Roberts are with Christ, speaking of things we only dream and imagine could be said about the richness of God's grace and work for us. He has sat down at the table of Abraham our father, to discourse with Roberts and others about the eternal richness of Jesus Christ who forever is seen in the eternal glimpse of God's glory for the saints in heaven. Yet, I will be content, for now, to take my grandfather's advice and read as much of Roberts as I can. Here is a brief outline of this godly man and his works.

Francis Roberts (1609-1675), a Presbyterian and Calvinistic Puritan, was born in Yorkshire in 1609. He was the son of Henry Roberts of Aslake. After his conversion to the Christian Gospel, and the desire to have a great interest in Christ, he proceeded to obtain degrees at Trinity College, Oxford in 1625 surrounding divinity. In 1632 he completed his degrees and was ordained to the Gospel ministry. Having been ordained and biblically guided to join the Presbyterian Church at the outbreak of the civil war, he also took *the Solemn League and Covenant*. In 1649 he was presented to the rectory of Wrington in Somersetshire by his patron Arthur lord Capel, son of the beheaded lord Capel. Later, he became minister of

St. Augustine, Watling-street.[1] While on this living he was appointed one of the commissioners for the "ejectment of those" who were called, "ignorant and insufficient ministers and schoolmasters." He went to Ireland with the Earl of Essex; and while there was made doctor of divinity.[2]

Roberts was a close friend and confidant of Robert Ballie, one of the Scottish Commissioners to the Westminster Assembly, and acted as an intermediary between the Scottish ministers and those of London.

Roberts died at Wrington about the end of 1675.

Roberts' principal theological work is entitled "Clavis Bibliorum, the Key of the Bible," in 2 volumes published in 1649; and again in folio in 1675. He also published, besides some single sermons, "The Believer's Evidence for Eternal Life," "The Communicant Instructed," "Mysterium et Medulla Bibliorum, or the Mystery and Marrow of the Bible;" and, "The True Way to the Tree of Life." His most popular work, received by the church at large, was *not* a book, but a

---

[1] He was a hearty Presbyterian Puritan and a minister at the parish of St. Augustine Watling Street during the time of the English Civil War.
[2] At the restoration, however, he conformed, tired out, as many others were, by the distractions of the contending parties, and disappointed in every hope which the encouragers of rebellion had held forth. It does not appear whether he had any additional preferment, except that of chaplain to his patron when Capel became earl of Essex; and when that nobleman was lord-lieutenant of Ireland in 1672, it is supposed he procured him the degree of B.D. at the University of Dublin.

theological chart called, "A Synopsis of Theology or Divinity."[3] It was specifically written to aid the people of his congregation to understand the basics of the Christian faith more precisely and easily by way of a visual aid. It is a masterful outline of theology and speaks to the congregation as Christians and not scholars.

Roberts *was* a scholarly writer. His *Clavis Bibliorum*, being an analysis of the contents of the Bible with annotations for students, and a preface by Calamy, was published in London, 1648, 8vo, and a portion of it at Edinburgh, 12mo, in the following year (3rd edition, London, 1665, 4to; 4th edition, 1675, fol.). Being dissatisfied with existing versions of the Psalms (the metrical psalter), he published anonymously, and without place or date, "The Book of Praises," (1644), an essay in translation containing Psalms 40-72. At the request of "judicious ministers and Christians," he included in the third edition of the "Clavis" an *entire* metrical version of the Psalms, those previously published by him as the, "Fourth Book of the Book of Hymns and Praises."

His portrait at the age of forty, engraved by Thomas Cross, is in the second edition of his, "A Communicant

---

[3] This amazing chart has been reproduced and published by Puritan Publications and can be found at the Puritan Shop, www.puritanshop.com.

Instructed" (published in 1651), and appears at the head of this introduction.

God's Afflicting Providence and Other Works

INTRODUCTION TO THE PROVIDENCE OF GOD

The Checker-work of God's Providences towards His Own People, Made up of Black and Whites

That is, of their abasements and advancements; their distresses and deliverances; their sullying tribulations and beautifying relaxations; represented in a sermon preached at the funeral of that faithful servant of the Lord, Mary the last wife of Joseph Jackson Esq., Alderman of the city of Bristol on the 5th day of May, 1657 A.D.

by Francis Roberts,
Pastor of the church at Wrington

"When he hath tried me, I shall come forth as gold,"
(Job 23:10).
"We must through much tribulation enter into the kingdom of God," (Acts 14:22).

LONDON,
Printed by *R.W.* for *George Calvert* at the sign of the *Half-moon* in Paul's Churchyard.
1657

To my much honored friend Joseph Jackson Esq., Alderman of the city of Bristol; as also, to all the entirely beloved children of Mary his late dear and gracious yoke-fellow, now sleeping in Jesus—yes—*living* with Jesus; grace, mercy, and peace from the Father of mercies and God of all consolation.

My Dear Christian friends,

When, upon your desires, I had preached the following sermon at the late sad funeral of such a wife, of such a mother, as you did not long have, I thought my work about this particular topic and situation had been at an end. Since which, through the importunity of diverse near and dear relations (whose requests to me are a virtual command) thinking better of it than I myself, I have been induced to publish it for the benefit of them and others who might read it in later years. My hope is that the good Lord would add his blessing both to what was then spoken and is now written, for furthering of their faith and helping of their joy. And now I present the sermon revised to you (and where it was needful I have enlarged it a little), who from her own designation, recommended the present text to me. The jewel in the words deserves a richer cabinet—yes—and her sacred dust a better monument. But until you meet with richer and better, let this be favorably accepted. (It was revised with the help of two distinct couples who heard the sermon taken in shorthand when I preached it just in case any useful passages should be omitted; and take note that there is a different gift in writing than there is in preaching.)

Not long since, I was (by reason of a continuing sickness and fever), not far from the hand of the grave; but the living God has loved my soul and lifted it from the pit of corruption so that in this sermon I have preached my own experiences and her expectations of deliverance. The gracious Lord (whose methods of mercy are many) has released us both from our respective extremities[4] as from the pots in our text, as well as me from death—that I might live to his praise a while on earth; her—by death—that she may live in his praise forever in heaven. God is three times blessed and the Father of mercies, for all the mysteries of his mercies.

May I now speak a few words of advice to you that survive; especially to you the dear and hopeful children of so happy a mother? My sincere love to her, my ardent longings after your salvation constrain me, and I cannot hold my peace. Let me stand a while as in your late mother's stead. O! let my counsel be accepted and embraced.

Become godly and religious now and afterwards. Know, fear, love, and serve God from your very youth.

---

[4] That is, from June 22 until almost July 20, 1656. Psalm 49:15, 68:13; Isa. 38:17.

Remember your Creator in the days of your youth. Early Christians are happy Christians. Under the Old Testament God called for the first-fruits of the ground, and the firstlings of the flock; much more he expects the firstlings of our days, of our youth and of our strength. Think of Samuel, David, Solomon, Obadiah, Josiah, John the Baptist, Timothy, and Jesus Christ himself; how religious they were in their very youth and you must tread in their steps. O! what sins and iniquities are prevented? What experiences of God are up-heaped; how large a seed time of grace and good works is obtained; how long opportunities of making our calling and election sure are enjoyed, by giving up ourselves to God in these days. (1 Chron. 28:9; 1 Kings 18:3, 12; Eccl. 12:1; Exod. 34:22, 26; Deut. 12:6, 17; 1 Sam. 3:4-21, 16:7, 11, 13, and 17:33; 1 Chron. 22:5, 29:1; 2 Sam. 12:24; 1 Kings 3:3, 28:3-12; 2 Chron. 34:1-3; Luke 1:15; 2 Tim. 3:15; Luke 2:40, 42, 46, 47, 52; 2 Peter 1:10).

2. Be *sincerely* and *entirely* religious. Hypocrisy is a mere mockery in religion; which occasions the deeper condemnation. Do not content yourselves with a name to live, but be alive indeed. Do not rest in the form, but look to the power of godliness. Serve the Lord with a perfect heart. Seek, love, and obey him with the whole heart. Let the whole soul be as it were dyed in grace. Fill your judgment with the knowledge and truth, your consciences with purity, your wills

with that which is easy to control, your hearts and affections with heavenliness, *etc.* Approve yourselves throughout to God that you may say as Peter, "Lord thou knowest all things, thou knowest I love thee," (John 21:17); say to him, I fear you, I trust in you, *etc.* (*cf.* Mark 23:14, 24:51; Rev. 3:1; 2 Tim. 3:5; 1 Chron. 18:9; Psalm 119:10).

3. Maintain sweet communion with God in Jesus Christ. Walk closely with God everyday as Enoch, Noah, Abraham, David, *etc.* Think of him frequently; desire him vehemently; love him entirely; never be well but in his presence. Accept all stirrings of his Spirit, glimpses of his face, tastes of his love. Open with him every morning, shut with him (like the sunflower) every night; turn towards him and pant after him all day long. Say, *whom have we in heaven but you?* In this way you shall recover the lost paradise; in this way you shall live as in a heaven on earth; and when you come to die, you shall simply exchange one heaven for another and a better—a spiritual heaven of grace for an eternal heaven of glory. (Gen. 5:22-24, 6:9, 17:2, and 48:15; Psalm 101:2; 1 Kings 15:5; Psalm 18:22; Acts 13:22; Psalm 73:25).

4. Let Jesus Christ be your all; your wisdom to guide you, your righteousness to justify you; your sanctification to clean you; your redemption to save you. If you hunger, he gives living water; if you faint, he is the consolation of Israel. If you

pray, he is an advocate with the Father; if you conflict with spiritual enemies, he is your hope. If you die, he is your gain; if you are buried also, he is your life and resurrection. O! let him be the Alpha and Omega, the center and the circumference—yes—the very all in all; your desires, loves, joys, delights, endeavors, and undertakings. If you lack Christ, you lack all things; if you have Christ, you lack nothing. In all your joys, Christ is the highest exultation; in all your sorrows, Christ is the sweetest consolation. In all your gains, Christ is the chief remuneration; in all your losses, Christ is the richest compensation. In him make up the loss of wife and mother, all sweetness, dearness, tenderness, fullness, contentment, satisfaction, consolation, and happiness is a thousand fold in him more than in these, or all the relations of the world. These are but glimmering lamps; he is the glorious Sun. These are but broken cisterns, he is the living fountain. These are but little drops, he is the boundless ocean. Now therefore, turn all your desires and affections towards him and be *fully* satisfied. One Christ is beyond ten thousand worlds. (1 Cor. 1:30; John 6:48-51, 4:10-14, 21:25; Luke 2:25; 1 John 2:1-2, 5:4-5; Rom. 8:37; 1 Tim. 1:1; Phil. 1:21; Rev. 8:11; Col. 3:11).

5. Strive after well-grounded assurance of a good spiritual state. Labor not only that God, Christ, grace, and glory may be yours; but also, that you may know assuredly they are yours. Assurance is possible, for God's Spirit is given

to help us to it. Many have attained it. Assurance is necessary, for God has charged us to endeavor after it; *give diligence to make your calling and election sure.* And assurance is very comfortable and advantageous to our perseverance. This held up Job under all his misery. This cheered up Paul against appearing death. (1 Cor. 2:12; Job 19:25-27; Heb. 10:34; 1 Tim. 1:16; 2 Tim. 1:12, 4:6-8; 2 Peter 1:10).

6. Contend exceedingly that grace may still be growing and sin is dying. The more grace and the less sin; the less like Satan, the more like God; the further from hell, the nearer to heaven. The abolition of sin and the perfection of grace are suburbs of glory. (2 Peter 3:18, Col. 3:5; Eph. 5:27, 4:12-13).

7. Live to God and upon God in Christ that you may live *with* God and *with* Christ. Live to God in all holy, heavenly, and blameless conversation; live upon God in all constant faithful dependence that you may live with God and Christ in immediate eternal enjoyments. (Rom. 14:8; Hab. 2:4; John 14:3, 19).

8. Live in love on to another and towards all God's people. Love entirely, love affectionately, love Christianly in order, chiefly to spiritual and eternal things. Sincere love is the badge and character of Christ's disciples on earth; and love will be part of the crown of Christ's members in heaven. O! you dear children that tumbled in the same bowels, still retain

the same mind, heart, and affection one towards another. You shall have adversaries enough in the world; and therefore, never be one another's adversaries. So live in love together on earth, as those that look to live in ravishments together in heaven. (1 John 4:7-8, John 13:34-35; 1 Cor. 13:13; Phil. 2:1-2).

9. Highly prize and frequent all the means of grace in public and private, for God's ordinances are his sacred channels in which alone his streams of grace ordinarily flow. How did David exult in the enjoyment of them! How did he lament in the want of them! Christians ought to observe Christ's commandments and ordinances. They must not forsake the assembling of themselves together, as the manner of some is. O! blessed is that people that know the joyful sound! The New Covenant and the administrations thereof are to continue until the end of this world; and therefore, they ought still to be attended upon by all God's New Covenant people. (Psalm 84:1, 122:1, 12:1-5, 63:1-2, 89:15; Mark 28:19-20; Heb. 10:25, 12:20; 1 Cor. 11:26, 15:58; Rev. 2:10; 2 John 8; 2 Thess. 3:13; Gal. 6:9).

10. Be constant, steadfast, persevering, and abounding in faith, obedience, and all goodness to the end. Be faithful to the death; then you shall receive a crown of life; then you shall receive a full reward. Do not be weary of well-being, for in due time you shall reap if you do not faint. How constant and steadfast to the end was your gracious mother in faith,

patience, and godliness, although no small tempest of pain and trouble laid upon her. The best of saints may be exercised with the worst of sorrows here; but the Lord is with them in the furnace of their trials—yes—was with her to uphold her in the valley of the shadow of death. Therefore, though she was troubled on every side, yet was she not distressed, though perplexed, yet not in despair; though cast down, yet not destroyed. We count them happy that endure. O! do not let the sharpest trials or troubles ever make you faint or plough, and look back, or render themselves unfit for the kingdom of God. (Dan. 2:25; Exod. 3:1; Isa. 43:2; Psalm 23:4; 2 Cor. 4:8; James 5:11; Luke 9:61).

11. Lastly, mourn moderately in the loss of her and other earthly comforts. When holy Jacob died in Egypt, the Israelites, the children of Jacob, mourned seven days, but the Egyptians seventy days. This was not because the Egyptians had more love to Jacob than the Israelites; but because the Israelites had more grace, hope, and moderation than the Egyptians. Natural affection is commended; excelling in mourning is condemned. Jesus himself wept at Lazarus's grave; and yet Christ's members must not mourn as others that do not have hope, for they that sleep in Jesus. If she was still lying among the sullying pots, in midst of her sighs, groans, dolors, and extremities, you might well bleed over her and lament her; but that she is delivered from all her sins and

sorrows, is as the wings of a dove, covered with silver, *etc.*, has laid aside her earthly fables and is clothed in heavenly white; is in Abraham's bosom in paradise with saints, angels, and with Jesus Christ our God, which is far best of all, *etc.* Now rejoice in her joys, triumph in her triumphs, she is not so much dead as *delivered* by death; she has (as Jerome said of Nepotianus) not so much lost her friends; as changed them and changed them for better; she is not so much unclothed, as clothed upon her mortality, being swallowed up of life. Let her have your imitations, rather than your lamentations. Her graces and gracious deportments towards God and man and more especially towards you; in her health and sickness, in her life, and at her death were very Christian and exemplary. In all, do follow her, as she followed Christ. Let her *virtues* still live in you; so shall she in some sense still live with you. And inasmuch as the resurrection of the dead is the peculiar hope and consolation of Christians, consider that she sleeps in Jesus, she shall at last awake and be raised again by Jesus. And you shall meet again; meet and never part; meet not to sigh and mourn altogether, but to sing and triumph together. You shall be caught up with her and with all the elect together, to meet the Lord in the air, and so shall you be ever with the Lord.[5] Amen. *So prays,*

---

[5] Gen. 50:3, 10; 1 Thess. 4:13, John 11:35; 1 Thess. 4:13-17; Luke 16:22, 23:43;

Your affectionate friend, and brother in the Lord, for the furtherance of your faith and joy,

Francis Roberts

Wrington, June 12, 1657.

Heb. 12:22-23; Phil. 1:23; 2 Cor. 5:4; 1 Cor. 11:1. *Intelligeres illum non emori, sedemigrare; et mutare amicos nontelinquere. Hieronym in Epitaph. Nepotian p. 25. Tom. I. Basil 1553. Fiduela Christianorum, resurrectio mortuorum. Tertul. de Resurrect. c. 1. p. 314.*

THE SERMON:
The Checker-work of God's Providences Towards His Own People, Made up of Blacks and Whites

That is, of their abasements and advancements; their distresses and deliverances; their sullying tribulations and beautifying relaxations, *etc.*

"Though ye have lien among the pots; yet shall ye be as the wings of a dove covered with silver, and her feathers with yellow gold," (Psalm 68:13).

God's dearest people may for a long time walk in darkness; yet at last the light of refreshing consolation shall shine upon them; may sit down with Job a great while among the ashes; yet at length shall be lifted up, God turning their captivity; and may lie with Israel (God's only people under the Old Testament) among the pots, for many ages; but shall safely escape, like silver-winged and golden-feathered doves, from all the blackish sulliedness of their afflictions. The sharpest storm ends in a grateful calm; and the darkest night has its succeeding day. This mercy here promised was (according to the purpose of the most high) performed to God's Israel. And this blessing, is in some sense, accomplished to our late dear sister deceased an Israelite indeed. This was her condition; she long walked in darkness; sat down with Job in ashes; and lay with Israel among the pots. But at last the gracious Lord has turned her darkness into light, her ashes into beauty, and her pots of sad affliction into glory. (Isa. 50:20; Job 19:8, 30:26, 2:8, 42:10; Psalm 18:27-28, 68:13; Gen. 15:17).

These words were first and immediately directed to the Jewish church, which had been a long time exercised with very many and heavy afflictions; but are extensive also, in like condition, to the Christian church which is incorporated into it and of the same body—yes—and applicable also, in a due rule of proportion to any particular Christian in a like parallel case of darkness of dark, distressing tribulations. A particular promise first directed to one single person is sometimes improved to the general consolation of Christians. As that sweet promise to Joshua—I will not fail you nor forsake you—is urged by the apostle as a general ground of contentment to all Christians in any troubles or oppositions. How much more may a general promise to the whole church, as here is applied to the comfort of a particular member. And therefore, I cannot but impute it to the Christian judgment and apprehensiveness of our deceased sister (now with the Lord) that she could appropriate the consolation of this more general promise to herself in particular; and that, though the sense and comfort of this promise is wrapped up and enfolded in obscure metaphorical expressions. The words were often in her heart and lips in the days of her tribulation; when doubtless she supported herself with pertinent and comfortable meditation. For (1) here she had (in the churches abject, blackish, deformed, and despised condition that had *lien among the pots*) a lively delineation of her own extreme distresses. And, if the whole church of God lay among the pots; why might not she? This might administer to her much matter of patience, contentedness, and consolation. It's some consolation, not to be alone in the heaviest tribulation. (2) Here she had (in the churches promised felicity that should be as the wings of a dove covered with silver and her feathers with yellow gold), a foundation of hope touching her deliverance at last out of all her extremities. If the church should be brought from her black sullying posts, to the wings of a silver and golden-colored dove; from darkest miseries to brightest felicities. Why might not she, in God's due time, one way or other, expect the like happy transmutation? This might sweetly nourish her faith, hope, and Christian expectation. This Scripture was so suitable to her condition, and so much in her thoughts, that discoursing about her expected dissolution, she said, "I think this must be the text at my funeral; though ye have lien among the pots, yet shall ye be as the wings of a dove covered with silver and her feathers with yellow gold." And hereupon, I have been requested, by some of her nearest relations, to make these words the subject matter of my discourse upon this sad occasion.[6]

This Scripture (and so this Psalm) is very mysterious and intricate; one thing being expressed, another intended; as is usual in metaphors and allegories. For removing the obscurity of the words and improving them to our present utility, we consider: (1) their coherence with the context; (2) their true sense and meaning, and (3) the lessons or doctrinal propositions intended in them. We must take more pains than ordinary to attain the right meaning of these words.

I. The coherence of these words with the context may be briefly represented as follows, that is,

Of this Psalm (most justly styled by Rabbi A. Ezra, a very excellent Psalm), (1) the penman, (2) matter, (3) occasion, and (4) parts are as follows:[7]

I. The instrumental author or penman was David, that sweet psalmist of Israel. See the title of the psalm. (2 Sam. 23:1)

II. The subject matter is of a mixed nature, being made up of petition and congratulation of doctrine and exhortation of history and prophecy, and containing such an eminent prophecy of Christ's triumphant ascension into heaven and of

---

[6] Eph. 3:6; Josh. 1:5; Heb. 13:5-6; Psalm 68:13. *Solomon miseris soclos habuisse Doloris.*

[7] *Non inter omnes convenit de argumento hujus Psalmi, quem affirmat Ezra valde esse excellentem. Sim. de Muis in arg. ad Psalm ixv ii.*

the benefits of it. You have ascended on high, you have led captivity captive—it may deservedly be ranked among the prophetical psalms. (Compare Psalm 68:18 with Eph. 5:8)

III. The occasion seems to be either (1) David's bringing up of the ark of God into the place prepared for it in Zion, in the city of David as some, or (2) some difficult and eminent expedition of David against his enemies; wherein he beforehand assures himself of desired success and victory, both from the assistant power of the mighty God and from Israel's constant experiences of like nature as others, or (3) some famous and renowned victory obtained as others, or (4)—as to me seems most probable—a complex series and heap of victories over this and his kingdom's enemies subdued under him, even from the Nile to the Euphrates, recorded in 2 Samuel 8 and 1 Chron. 18, on which he is by some supposed to have penned two triumphant psalms, that is, Psalm 47:5 and Psalm 68:18. In this, King David, being a special type of Christ, who is the King of Kings that subdues all our spiritual enemies and captivates our captivity, as part of this psalm applied to and interpreted of Christ is clearly intimated. And throughout the whole flow of this psalm, besides its immediate literal sense touching David and his temporal kingdom, there is easily observable a mediate, spiritual, and mystical meaning touching Christ the true David and his spiritual kingdom. Let this be remembered except we lose much of the spirituality of this heavenly psalm. (Compare Psalm 68:1 with Num. 10:35, as that in 2 Sam. 21:15-22. See also Psalm 68:1-2, Psalm 68:18 with Eph. 4:8).

IV. The parts or branches are chiefly three, that is, (1) petition, (2) exhortation, (3) congratulation.

1. A prophetical petition—*let God arise, etc.* (ver. 1-3). This was the prayer at the moving of the ark, that singular token of God's presence, type of Jesus Christ, and glory in Israel, (Num. 10:35; Exod. 25:21-22; 1 John 2:2; Rom. 9:4; 1 Sam. 4:21-22).

2. A pathetic exhortation or hortatory incitation to the high praises of God, (ver. 4-19).

3. A grateful exultation in the Lord for his many blessings and victories, (verse 19 to the end).

This 13th verse falls under the second branch, that is, the exhortation. The psalmist exhorts to the praises of God from two sorts of motives especially, that is (I) from God's more general and common acts of providence, (1) to the fatherless, (2) to the widows, (3) to the solitary, and (4) to the captives (ver. 4-6); and (II) from God's more special and peculiar providences towards his own people Israel. And this is chiefly done in four observable intervals of time that came over them, that is, (1) when they came out of Egypt and marched through the wilderness, (ver. 7-8); (2) when they were newly possessed of and planted in the land of Canaan, (ver. 9-10), (3) when in the troublesome and unsettled times of the judges, (ver. 11-12), and (4) when in the more composed and happy days of David, (ver. 13-19). In this last particular note two things, *that is,*

(1) The preface to this matter of praise and thankfulness for God's providential goodness which should be to Israel in the days of David more than in former times, *though you have lien among the pots; yet, you shall be as the wings of the dove covered with silver, etc.,* (ver. 13). That is, in the three former times in Egypt and the wilderness, in Canaan, and under the judges—you have *lain as among the pots*—low, debased, blacked, deformed, *etc.*, with many and sore afflictions. But now under David's dominion, especially under Christ's—you shall be as dove's wings, and feathers of silver and golden color; you shall escape and be delivered, you shall be advanced to a more joyous, prosperous, and happy condition and have better times than ever formerly. You shall be taken from among the pots and adorned with opposite beauty and glory.

(2) The particular arguments inciting Israel to praise and thankfulness hereupon are drawn, (i) from God's victories over his enemies to his people's prosperity, (ver. 14); (ii) from the eminency and fertility of God's hill, Zion, especially of the church of God shadowed out by it, (ver.15); (iii) from the Lord's constant residence in and all-sufficient protection of

his own hill,(is that right?, will?) his church and people, (ver. 16-17), and (iv) from God's triumph over all his and his people's enemies, which was to have its chief accomplishment in Jesus Christ ascending up into heaven and leading captivity captive, (ver. 18). In this way stands the coherence by which you may receive much satisfaction touching the right meaning of the words. (Eph. 4:8)

II. The sense and meaning of the words will now be the more easily extracted. Here's one Hebrew word in the original which especially renders the Scripture intricate, that is, שְׁפַת *shawfath*, which, being a word of diverse significations and transactions, occasions various interpretations. It is rendered (1) limits or bounds, (2) lots or inheritances, and (3) pots or pot ranges.

(1) Some render it, two limits or two bounds, (the word being of the dual number), that is, the two limits, bounds or coasts of the enemies, ready to afflict, vex, and infest them on each hand. Or, two confines of the country where they fortified themselves against their enemies. This sense some later writers embrace, and it's one of the interpretations which Henry Ainsworth gives, though not in the first place. But this version seems here very unsuitable; for that it quite destroys the elegancy and fitness of the

opposition between the two metaphors representing Israel's different conditions before and under David's government.[8]

(2) Some render it two lots or two inheritances. So the Septuagint, ἐὰν κοιμηθῆτε ἀνὰ μέσον τῶν κλήρων πτέρυγες περιστερᾶς περιηργυρωμέναι καὶ τὰ μετάφρενα αὐτῆς ἐν χλωρότητι χρυσίου διάψαλμα; that is, amidst the lots or between the inheritances; inheritances (as in Canaan) being anciently set out by lots. This Jerome seems to follow, turning it, *si dormiatis inter medios cleros*. And in this way he expounds it, *when you believe the two testaments, in both you shall find the Holy Spirit*. And though there is a beauty, even according to the letter to know what you read; yet the force of all the comeliness is in the sense. Therefore, the outward ornament of the words is demonstrated by the name of silver, but the more secret mysteries are contained in the hidden gifts of gold, *etc*. So that with him, the two lots are the two testaments; the dove is the Holy Spirit; her wings covered with silver, the outward letter of the testament; the feathers of yellow gold, the inward, spiritual, and mysterious sense. But this is rather a

---

[8] To this effect Mercerus and Cevalerius in S. *Pagnin. Thess.* add it as a verb, and Moller. Com. in Psalm 68. Or, we may understand it of the two bounds and limits of the enemies where they are continually assailed and endangered. And this in the Greek seems to favor, turning it [*ana meson loon clercon amids* (or between)] the inheritances; even as they also translate the two burdens or limits between which Issachar couched, (Gen. 49:14), which tribe had the Philistines at one end and the Ammonites on the other, that vexed them. H. Ainsworth in his *Annotat*. in Psalm 68:14.

witty allegorical allusion than a judicious and solid exposition. St. Augustine also expounds the words much to this effect: but altogether this is unsatisfactorily. The ancient fathers are not always the best expositors.[9]

But most render the words *pots* or *pot ranges*. So, although here you have *lain among the pots* (or between the pot ranges, or between the two banks or rows, that is, of stones to hang posts on in the camp or league) yet you shall be as the wings of a dove covered (or decked with silver and her feathers with yellow-greenish gold). And they observe in the words a double metaphor: (1) the one, of Israel's lying among the pots as scullions lie among the pots, kettles, or cauldrons in the camp or league in time of war and so are blackened, soiled, smutted, deformed; denoting Israel's abject, low, mean, sullied, deformed, and despicable condition under afflictions and extreme distresses in time past in Egypt, the wilderness, Canaan, and in the time of the judges. And then, (2) the other of Israel's being like the wings of a dove (which is of very speedy flight for escape) of bright silver and beauteous golden

---

[9] *Si dormiatis inter medios cleros, etc. Cum doubus crediderls Testamentis, invenics in ut toque Spiritum Sanctum. Et dicet sit pulchritudo etiam juxta literam scire que legas; amen vis lecoris omnis in sensu est. Exterator itaq; verborum ornatus in Argenti nomine demostratur, occultiora vero mysteria in reconditis juri muneribus continentur. Si dormiatis inter medios cleros; hoc est, si quiescatis inter novum ... us Testamentum invenietis in duobus Testamenti; graclum Spiritus Sancti. Cleri licuntur singuli liberi, etc.* Hieronym in *Gomment.* ad Psalm.lxvii. page 94 B.C. *Tom.* 8 Basil 1553. St. Augustine in *Enarrat.* in Psalm lxvii p. 702, *etc. Tom* 8 Basil, 1569.

color; representing their escape and deliverance at last out of all their blacking, smutting and deforming afflictions, into the contrary, beauteous, prosperous and happy state, under the kingdom of David, especially of Jesus Christ *the true David*. *Blackness* notes extreme affliction and misery. *Dove's wings* means *escape*; white silver-color and beauteous golden color, mean *prosperity* and *felicity*. So, the metaphors are elegantly opposed one to another, and very significantly set forth the several conditions of Israel, first as lying among the pots of deep afflictions in former times, but after as assured of deliverance, of better days and that they should be as a silver winged and golden feathered dove, full of beauty, comeliness, prosperity, and felicity. To this effect, R. David Kimchi, Pagnin, Calvin, Muis, Foord, Ainsworth, and others expounds these words. And in my judgment this exposition seems most genuine and proper; as being without forcing, most agreeable both to the intent of the context and propriety of the words. And in this way they are very suitable to this present sad occasion.[10] Between the pot ranges, or between the two banks

---

[10] Psalm 51:6-7; R. David in Comment. *Sunt...; Chytropodes, loca ubi ponuntur ollae, aut caldariae. In loco humili, et nigro, ut est his locus. Ac si dicat, si ambulastis hactenus nigris induti vestibus ob inimicorum afflictionem, adhuc eritis albi sicut alae columbae, quae tecti est argento. Quae habet pennas albas sicut argentum. S. Pagnin in the four ad verb... Inter Chytropedes. In loco humili, sictu est locus chytropodum; vel in loco obscure et atro. In summa anxietate et rebus adversis constitenti fuerit es. Eritis adhue sicut Pennae columbae tectae argento, Candor faelicitatem significat. Pag et Mercer ib. Nunc per modum correctionis addit, etiam se fideles inderdum contingat*

or rows, in other words, of stones made to hang pots and kettles on in the camp or league; places where scullions lie, and so are black; meaning by this affliction and misery; as on the contrary, by the doves silver-rings is meant prosperity. This is how Mr. Ainsworth answers this in his *Annotat.* on Psalm 68:14. He says, *Though ye have*—the meaning is after that you, O people of God, shall for a long time have endured base slavery and have been like scullion boys lying upon the ground, dirty and smoky; you shall be again restored to glory and honor by God's deliverance. John Diodati in his *Annot.* on Psalm 68:14 says, that *Among the pots*—means that though God suffers his church for a time to lie in darkness, like a black

---

jucere in tenebris, Deum nihilominus in tempore prodire liberatotrem. Generaliter admonet, inter medias afflictiones arcana et mirisica Dei vertute fideles quasi intergros servari, vel subito restitual, ut nulla malorum signa appareant. Utrumque enim sensum verba admittunt; Quod jacentes in suligine et tenebris, nitere tamen non desinant; Vel quod liberatio contractum ex amlis nigredinem discutiat. Utrum vis Ieligas, summa huc tedit, numquam afficionibus vel consumi vel obrui fideles, quin sua illis maneat incolumicas et Joan Calvin in Comment ad Psalm 68:14. In priore membro metaphora est a colinibus et lixis castrensibus petira, qui ab aeris injuria utcunque se defendunt, delitescendo inter fuliginosas ollas, et lapides focarlos, iapta huic loco, ubi de bello Sermo est figura. In posteriore est metaphora a Columbis desumpta, quae per medium acrem volitantes, nunc niveum atque argenicum, nunc aureum splendorem ejaculanture. Significantur porro hos, verse ex omnibus angust iis et periculis, quantumvis ingentibus, emersuros exhurosq; salvos et incolumes. In sacris literis Atror finala; Candor ver, incolumitatem et prosperitatem notat. Simeon de Muis in commnet. ad Psalm 68:14. Quamvis antea jacueritis, etc. Quamvis tribus predictis temporibus, in Egypto et Deserto, Interra Cananes, et sub judicubus fueritis hactenus similes Calonibus et lixis fuligine deformatis; deinceps tamen eritis simile; penni columbae, nunc sub imperio Davidis ampliorem habebant letandi occasionem quant unquam antea, et Joan Foord in Expos. Psalm 68:14.

scullion among the pots; yet he will restore it and make it most shining and bright.[11]

The words, in this way, explained are (1) narrative and (2) promissory. For here's (1) a narrative of Israel's former deep affliction and misery; *although you have lain among the pots.* They had been in former times in Egypt, the wilderness, Canaan, and under the judges, as so many scullions among the pots, abased, smutted, spotted, made black and deformed with many and great tribulations.

2. A promise of Israel's future deliverance, prosperity, and felicity; *yet shall you be as the wings of a dove, covered with silver, and her feathers with yellow gold.* They should not always lie blacked and sullied in the smoke and among the pots, they shall be as the wings of a dove, speedily escaping, they shall be delivered out of their dark and black condition and be made bright, beauteous, and every way prosperous, as white silver-colored and yellow-greenish-golden feathered dove; most ornate, pleasant, and beauteous.

III. The third thing that remains is, the observation of the doctrinal position, or lessons, which are intended here. The words are something like the cloudy pillar in the wilderness, which had a black side, full of darkness, (Exod. 24:29), and a bright side, full of light. In the black side we may

---

[11] Large London. *Annotat.* on Psalm 68:13

read this lesson that sometimes God's Israel, God's own endeared people, may lie, as it were among the pots, in deepest distresses and afflictions. In the bright side, on the other hand, we may read this instruction; that God's distressed and afflicted people shall not always lie among the pots, but at last, as with dove's wings, escape out of all their distress and misery and enjoy all contrary mercy, prosperity, and felicity.

Let me speak a little briefly to both of these observations, which notably set forth the diversity of God's dispensations towards his own people; as it were the checkerwork of God's providence to them. We see clearly their black and white conditions; God will abase them by difficult and lingering tribulations, and afterwards He will advance them by beautifying relaxations.

DOCTRINE 1: That sometimes God's Israel, God's own endeared people, may lie as it were among the pots in deepest distresses and afflictions.

This doctrinal lesson is evidently fluent from the first branch of the text. For unfolding and improving of this I will chiefly manifest it to you in the following way. (1) That God's people being in deep distresses and afflictions are likely to be among the pots. (2) *Why* God suffers his church and dearest people sometimes in this way to lie as among the pots in deepest distresses and tribulations. (3) What inferences may readily result upon this.

I. That the lying of God's endeared people in deepest distresses and afflictions is like lying among the pots. *For,*

1. They that lie among the pots are in a very low, mean, and abject condition; scullions of the meanest rank are accustomed in the camp or league to lie among the pots. So they that are in deep distresses and afflictions are in a very low, mean, and abject state in the eye of the world. Israel, in affliction, was in a very low condition—who remembered us in our low estate. Low in Egypt, when they toiled in the clay and must make brick without straw. Low at the Red Sea, when nothing but present death was before their eyes. Egyptians being behind them, the sea before them, and mountains on each hand. Low in the wilderness, when they had neither bread to eat, nor water to drink, *etc.* Low in the land of Canaan, when they were delivered into their enemies hands, which swarmed about them like bees—yes—when the ark of God was taken from them—yes—when Saul and Jonathan were destroyed. Low in Babylon, when they were visibly as helpless and hopeless as people dead and buried in their very graves. So Joseph was very low in his affliction, when he was shackled up in prison in Egypt and laid in irons, having not one friend in all Egypt to help him out. Job was very low, when smitten with sore boils from the sole of his

foot to the crown of his head so that he scraped himself with a potsherd and sat down among the ashes. David was very low, when he in fear of his life, changed his behavior, feigning himself mad before Achish king of Gath; and when he fled from Absalom his son, going up Mount Olivet barefoot, weeping, and having his head covered, *etc.* Jonah was very low, when he was as it were twice buried, once in the sea and again in the belly of the whale, and the weeds were wrapped about his head. And Lazarus extremely low, when he lay hunger-bitten, full of sores and ulcers at the rich man's gate, desiring his crumbs, which none gave to him, the dogs coming and licking his sores. (Psalm 136:23; Exod. 1:13-14, 5:10-11, 14:1-12, 16:3, & 17:1-3; Judg. 4:3 – see that whole book; 1 Sam. 4:11-22, 31:7; Ezek. 37:11-13; Gen. 39:20; Psalm 105:18; Job 2:7-8; Psalm 34 title; 1 Sam. 21:11-15; 2 Sam. 15:30; Jonah 1:15-17, 2:2-7; Luke 16:20-21).

    2. They that lie among the pots are apt to be spotted, sullied, fouled, blacked with the pots. So they that are in deep affliction and distress are rendered in the eyes of others, deformed, sullied, black, tanned, sunburned, *etc.* The afflicted church confesses: *I am black as the tents of Kedar. Even as the black hair-cloth, weather-beaten tests of Kedar.* And again—*look not upon me because I am black because the sun has looked upon me.* Great afflictions make the very church herself black or blackish and

sunburned; how much more her particular members? In this way Jeremiah lamented, "Our skin was black like an oven because of the terrible famine," (Lam. 5:10). "The Nazarites visage is blacker than a coal," (Lam. 4:7-8). Yes, our blessed Savior Jesus Christ himself was in his comeliness, deformed and marred, extraordinarily by his sore afflictions and sufferings. His visage was so marred more than any man, and his form more than the sons of men. He has no form nor comeliness, and when we shall see him, there is no beauty that we should desire him, (Job 30:30; Song of Solomon 1:5-6; Isa. 52:14, 53:2).

3. They that lie among the pots, being deformed, sullied, and blacked are accustomed to be slighted, despised, and abhorred; men look strange at them, are ashamed of their company and cannot abide to come near them. So they that lie in deep distress and misery are usually neglected, despised, and rejected of others. Yes, often times their very kindred, friends, and familiar acquaintances are estranged from them and stand aloof from their calamity. In this way Job in his extreme afflictions complained, "He hath put by brethren far from me, and mine acquaintance are verily estranged from me. My kinsfolk have failed, and my familiar friends have forgotten me. They that dwell in mine house, and my maids, count me for a stranger; I am an alien in their sight. I called my servant, and he gave me no answer; I entreated him with my

mouth. My breath is strange to my wife; though I entreated for the children's sake of mine own body. Yea, young children despised me; I arose, and they spake against me. All mine inward friends abhorred me; and they whom I loved are turned against me," (Job 19:13-22). So Heman the Ezrahite in his sad afflictions laments, "Lover and friend hast thou put far from me, and mine acquaintance into darkness," (Psalm 88:18). And, though our blessed Savior does not bear his own, but our griefs and our sorrows, yet even for them he was exposed to extreme contempt. "He is despised and rejected of men, a man of sorrows, and acquainted with grief; and we hid as it were our faces from him; he was despised, and we esteemed him not," (Isa. 53-3-6). O, how hard a thing is it for the dearest of God's saints to be deeply distressed and to be greatly despised!

II. But, why is it that the Lord suffers his church and his own endeared people, to lie sometimes in this way, as among the pots, in deepest distress and tribulations?

The Lord permits, orders, directs, and overpowers the sharp afflictions and distresses of his own dear people for their manifold benefit. He lets them lie among the pots that even this may turn to their profit and cooperate for their good, for their manifold good, (Heb. 12:10; Phil. 1:19; Rom. 8:28). *For,*

1. By these the sins and failings of God's people are more clearly detected. He does not withdraw his eyes from

the righteous; and if they are bound in fetters and held in cords of affliction, then he shows them their work and their transgressions that they have exceeded. The distress of Joseph's brothers in Egypt, revived afresh upon their consciences, their old offences against Joseph. Afflictions awaken their sleepy souls and drown consciences. As the sun's eclipse is best discerned in water, or as blots run most abroad in wet paper, so their sinful blots and eclipses are most evidently discovered in their waters of affliction, (Job 36:7-9; Gen. 41:21-22).

    2. By these they are more thoroughly melted and humbled for their sinful failings discovered. The fire melts the metal in the furnace so that it will run into any mold. When wrath was upon good Hezekiah for the pride and lifting up of his heart, how quickly he humbled himself under the hand of God! That phoenix King Josiah exceedingly melted and wept before the Lord when he discerned the judgments of God but hanging over their heads for sin in the clouds of the threatenings, (2 Chron. 32:24-26; 2 Chron. 35:16-17).

    3. By these—their spots, stains, and sins, detected and lamented, are very notably cleansed, rubbed out, and purged away. "By this shall the iniquity of Jacob be purged, and this is all the fruit to take away his sin," (Isa.17:8-9). David himself acknowledged this advantage by his afflictions, "But now have I kept thy word," (Psalm 119:67). So true is that of Elihu to Job,

"Then he openeth their ear to discipline, and commandeth that they return from iniquity," (Job. 6:8-10). Our afflictions lance out our corruption; scour away our spots and stains; file off our rust and canker; fan away our chaff; segregate our dross; and like the fiery furnace, burn off the bands and cords of our corruptions, that we may walk at liberty. Even Manasseh, that monster of wickedness, when taken among the horns and bound in fetter, *etc.*, repented and reformed, (2 Chron. 33:1-20; Dan. 3:23-25).

4. By these, their graces are tried and proved to show whether they are sincere; not that God does not know what is in us, but that we do not know what is in ourselves. "Think it not strange concerning the fiery trial, which is to try you," (1 Peter 4:11). "That the trial of your faith being much more precious than of gold that perisheth, though it be tried with fire, might be found unto praise, and honor, and glory," (1 Peter 1:6-7). Some writing cannot be read but at the fire or in the water. So some gracious endowments and inscriptions on our hearts, as faith, patience, self-denial, *etc.*, cannot so well be discerned as in the fire and water of tribulations. The furnace tries the metal; the touchstone tries the gold; the storm tries the pilot; the battle tries the soldier; so the furnace, touchstone, storm, and battle of afflictions *try* the faith, patience, courage, constancy, and graces of the Christian. Our

true spiritual beauty becomes the more beauteous by this washing, when thereby paint and counterfeit colors are wiped away.

5. By these, their graces and spirituals are much advanced and improved, as the body by a growing ague, or as the grass by an April shower. "Tribulation worketh patience, and patience experience, and experience hope, and hope makes not ashamed," (Rom. 5:3-5). What a rich and strange crop is this! Here grapes on thorns and figs on thistles. By rubbing, the pomander smells far sweeter; by treading the chamomile grow better; by wearing the nail becomes brighter; so our spirituals become more bright and fragrant, and flourishing, by being exercised with afflictions. Opposition and difficulties excite their activities. Had not the afflictions of Job been so extreme, the integrity and patience of Job would have not been so renowned, (Job 2:3, 9-10 with Lam. 5:11).

6. By these, their spiritual activity in meditations, prayer, self-examinations, self-denial, obedience and all Christian duties, is exceedingly actuated and awakened. When Jacob was in fear and danger of destruction by his brother Esau, he wrestled all night by prayer with an angel of the covenant and would not let him go with a blessing, (Gen. 32:24-26). While David was exercised under Saul's oppressive persecution and other sad afflictions, he breathed out to God

his most celestial devotions. Then he said, "It's good for me that I have been afflicted that I might learn thy statutes," (Psalm 119:71). When David was lowest in affliction, he was highest in devotion. Yes, Jesus Christ himself being in agony prayed more earnestly, (Luke 22:44). As the birds in the spring sing most sweetly when it rains most sadly; or as a musical instrument, when the strings are struck, sounds most melodiously. So when God rains down troubles upon us, and by his chastisements strikes the very springs of our hearts, often times our spirits make the sweetest melody in the ears of God.

7. By these they are conformed to Jesus Christ their head and elder Brother, who was a man of sorrows, acquainted with grief and perfected, or consecrated, *through sufferings*. And if we suffer with him, we shall be glorified together. If now we are conformed to him in his cross, we shall hereafter be conformed to him in his crown. It's the perfection of the members to be conformed to their head, (Rom. 8:8, 29-30; Isa. 53:2-4; Heb. 2:9-10, 8:7).

8. By these, their childlike relation to the heavenly Father is sweetly ascertained, while they are enabled to bear and endure his chastisements with filial patience and submission. "If ye endure chastening, God dealeth with you as with sons: for what son is he whom the Father chasteneth not? But if ye be without chastisement, whereof all are

partakers, then are ye bastards and not sons," (Heb. 11:6-8). The heavenly Father will take pains with his own children to chastise, discipline, and nurture them for their good; when he will not wear his rods upon bastards and castaways. And how useful is that his paternal affliction, which describes his fatherly affection to us, and our Son-like relation to him! I am well contented to be under the rod of the Almighty, so that I may be distinguished from the bastards of this world and numbered among the sons of God.

9. By these they are chastened of the Lord that they should not be condemned with the world. And that's a happy castigation that helps to prevent eternal condemnation. Who would not say with him: Here burn me, here cut me, that you may forever spare me? (1 Cor. 11:32; *Hic ure, his sera; ut in aeternum parcas.*)

10. Finally, by these sharp afflictions and distresses, God fits and prepares his afflicted servants for their eternal glory. Christ was first abased before he was exalted and passed by his cross to his crown, through his sufferings into his glory. And his members must follow him, "Through much tribulations we must enter into the kingdom of God," (Acts 14:22). We shall meet with tribulation, much tribulation; that's the way we must go, but through this much tribulation we must enter into the kingdom of God, that's the blessed end of this way. If it were tribulation and much tribulation, and

after that no entrance into heaven, that would be *the tribulation of tribulation*, a doleful way to a more doleful journey's end; but in that through this tribulation—yes—through this much tribulation, we shall at last enter into a kingdom, and that the kingdom of God. This renders all our tribulations as in effect no tribulation at all. And, "the momentary lightness of our affliction worketh for us a far more exceeding eternal weight of glory," (2 Cor. 4:17).[12] Our afflictions work this transcendent glory for us by working and disposing us for this transcendent glory. And the sharper our sorrows are here, the sweeter our joys will be hereafter. As health is most acceptable after the sharpest sickness, liberty most sweet after rigorous bondage, rest most delightful after toilsome weariness, and the harbor most welcome after the sorest storms. So heaven and glory itself will be most grateful and glorious after sharpest afflicting extremities. So, we have the causes why the Lord suffers his people to lie among the pots, (Eph. 4:9-10; Luke 24:26).

III. Inferences or corollaries from this resulting doctrine are diverse. *As,*

1. Here, behold the mystery and wisdom of God's providential dispensations. His own people (though his jewels) shall lie among the pots and be most sadly afflicted

---

[12] .*Greek from hyperbole to hyperbole, or a hyperbolical to hyperbolical.*

when the wicked shall flourish like a green bay tree in all prosperity. This strange dispensation of God's providence exceedingly puzzled and perplexed holy David until he went into the sanctuary of God; then he saw the end of those wicked prosperous men, that they were set in slippery places—that they are brought into desolation as in a moment, *etc.* Godly Lazarus lay full of sores among the dogs at the rich man's gate, destitute of his very crumbs to satisfy his hunger; while the wicked rich man was in his purple and fine linen and fared sumptuously every day (Psalm 73:1-21; Luke 16:19-21). Assuredly *then,*

(1) No man knows God's peculiar love or hatred by these external dispensations (Eccl. 9:1-2).

(2) Happiness or misery does not consist in having or lacking of these outward blessings; nor in escaping or enduring the sharpest sorrows or afflictions.

2. Therefore, saddest extremities of outward afflictions and miseries in this present life are not inconsistent with the gracious condition of God's own people. Yes, most usually God's own people in this world are of all others the most afflicted when as others enjoy the pleasures of sin for a season, (Heb. 11:26-27). O! what extremities of sufferings and deaths have the faithful undergone in all ages! Consult that little book of martyrs in the epistle to the Hebrews, "They were tortured, not accepting deliverance, that they might obtain a

better resurrection. And others had trial of cruel mockings and scourings, yea moreover of bonds and imprisonment. They were stoned: they were sawn asunder; were tempted; were slain with the sword; they wandered about in sheepskins, and goatskins being destitute, afflicted, tormented. Of whom the world was not worthy; they wandered in deserts, and in mountains, and in dens and caves of the earth," (Heb. 11:35-38).

O! what strange similitudes, emblems, and expressions are used in Holy Scripture for representing of God's people's calamities! As,

A smoking furnace to denote the affliction of Abraham's seed in Egypt, (Gen. 15:13, 17).

A bush burning with fire, all on a light flame to express Israel's former and future sharp and fiery calamities, (Exod. 3:2-3).

Their souls being bowed down to the dust and their bellies cleaving to the earth, (Psalm 44:25).

Their being sore broken in the place of dragons and covered with the shadow of death.

Yes, the Jews in Babylon's captivity said, "Our bones are dried, and our hope is lost, we are cut off for our parts," (Ezek. 37:11-14). And they were as so many dead bodies that were buried in their very graves. And therefore, extremity of distresses in this present life is not only consistent with, but very incident to, the sincerest heirs by grace of the life to come.

3. Therefore, let Christians learn patiently and contentedly to bear their heaviest pressures and afflictions, since no temptation has befallen them, but what is humane, (1 Cor. 10:13). Yes, sometimes it is the lot of the church of God, and of his dearest people, to lie even among the blackest pots. See, Joseph bound in irons; see Job sitting in the ashes; see Lazarus lying among the dogs full of sores; and consider Jesus Christ himself so full of sorrows; and do you think much at your own afflictions? O! do not fret against God's dispensations, do not faint, but endure your tribulations since Jesus Christ himself and his choicest members are here in these things your companions, (Psalm 105:18; Job 2:7-8; Luke 16:20-21; Isa. 53:2-4).

4. Therefore, how unsafe and imprudent is it to despise, abhor, or censure others of hypocrisy, or of nullity of grace, because of their sad, doleful, and strange afflictions! For, in so doing, we may rashly condemn the generation of the righteous, before we are aware. God's own endeared people often times lie among these blacking pots. O! think of David and all his afflictions, how he was hunted as a partridge and down the mountains, how all the day long he was plagued and chastened every morning; of Paul in perils and distresses on every side; of Jeremiah cast into the miry dungeon and (as

some think) sinking up to the armholes of the mire; of Daniel flung into the filthy and fatal den of the hungry lions; of the prophets persecuted and slain by the Jews, (Acts 7:52); of the three Jews bound hand and foot and cast into the hot burning fiery furnace, heated seven times hotter than ordinary for not worshipping the golden image; of Job covered all over with sore boils from the sole of his foot to his crown. Jerome thinks that Satan left only his tongue free that there he might blaspheme his Lord; of Lazarus full of sores and ulcers; of Hezekiah smitten with a mortal boil; of the godly killed all the day long and counted as sheep for the slaughter; of the martyrs, (Heb. 11:35); of the cruel primitive persecutions; and of Jesus Christ himself the spotless Son of God put to death and crucified by wicked hands and hung (for the greater infamy) between two thieves upon the cursed tree. O! think deliberately upon these instances, that is, of the unquestionable—yes, incomparable—piety of their persons and of the unutterable extremities of their passions and then take heed of the error of Job's friends, of despising, abhorring, or censuring any of the servants of Lord, though lying among the pots, though plunged under heaving, unusual, and extreme calamities. Do you think worse of a piece of gold because it is smeared with mud? Or do you ever less value a jewel because it's fallen into the dirt? It's gold still, though darkened; it's a rich jewel still, though bemired. Why then should we harbor more hard, mean, despising, undeserving, undervaluing thoughts of afflicted David, Paul, Job, Lazarus, or of any of the distressed saints of God; which in God's account are precious than gold still, or rich jewels still, though besmeared and blacked with most deforming and amazing miseries?[13]

5. Therefore, finally, behold one noted difference between the condition of God's people in earth and in heaven. Here God's endeared people may lie among the pots; may be smutted, soiled, blacked, *etc.*, in the eyes of men with deep and sore afflictions. But when once the last messenger has summoned them, and when once they shall set foot in heaven, they shall never lie among the pots anymore; they shall never be tanned with misery or sunburned with affliction anymore. But they shall perfectly rest from all their labors, of sins, temptation and tribulation. Then, no more sea, no more pain, no more crying, no more tears, *etc.* Then Job that here sat down among the ashes shall there set up among the angels. Then Lazarus that here lay among the dogs shall there be lodged in Abraham's bosom. Then the endeared saints and

---

[13] Psalm 132:1, 73:14; 2 Cor. 11:2-33; Jer. 38:6; Dan. 6:16-17, 3:21-23; Job 2:7-8; *A planta pecis usq; ad viticem percassit eum vulnere pessimo, H.H. Elephantia. Inae toto corpore vermis fluebunt, et sinles et putredo. Solam linguam integram ei reservavi, ut possi Dominum tuu ii blasphemare, Heirnyr. in comment ad Psalm 66. p. 92. D. Tom.* Luke 16:20; Rom. 8:6; Acts 2:23; Gal. 3:13; *Lucet margaritam in sordibus; et fulgor gemmae putissimae etiam in luto radiat. Heronym. ad Pammach. consol. p.164.c. Tom. 1. Basil 1553.*

servants of God that here often times lay among the pots shall walk with Christ in triumphant white and be counted worthy, (Song of Solomon 1:5-6; Rev. 14:13; Job 2:7-8; Luke 10:36, 16:20-22; Rev. 3:4).

And so I pass from the dark to the bright side of the text; yet shall you be as the wings of a dove covered with silver, *etc.* Here, *make note,*

DOCTRINE 2: That God's afflicted and distressed people shall not always lie among the pots, but at last (as with dove's wings) shall escape out of their deepest misery and enjoy all contrary mercy, prosperity, and felicity.

They may for a time lie in distress, but not always. Their outward misery may be great, but shall have an end. They may for a few years be oppressed in Egypt and wander in the wilderness, but at last they shall come to Canaan, the promised rest. Weeping by a lodge for a night, but shouting for joy in the morning. In a little wrath God may hide his face from his own for a moment, but with everlasting kindness will he have mercy on them. For a season they may lie among the pots, like black, soiled, and deformed scullions; but at length they shall be as the wings of a dove, covered with silver and her feathers with yellow gold. That is, they shall escape; escape harmless; escape beauteous, happy, and prosperous. Consider well the expressions in the text, that is, (1) *they shall escape*. This is noted by *wings*. They shall be (not as a dove, but) as the wings of a dove. Wings are swift; a dove's wings are eminently swift. By this the Scripture sets forth a swift and speedy escape from distress and trouble. David says, "O that I had wings like a dove, then would I flee away and be at rest," (Psalm 55:6-8). So, they that lie among the pots shall at last be as the wings of a dove; they shall have a way of escape, (1 Cor. 10:13). (2) They shall escape harmless and innocent. Why else does he mention the wings of a dove, rather than of any other fowl? Doves are commended by our Savior for their simplicity and harmlessness; *be wise as serpents and harmless* (or unmixed) *as doves*. God's people, when they are tried in the furnace of affliction, shall come forth as refined gold and silver. They shall be purified and made white and tried. They shall leave their dross behind them. (3) This is not all. For, they shall so escape out of distresses as to enjoy the contrary mercies and felicities. This seems to be imported in the dove's white, silver-colored, and golden-colored feathers; or, as the Hebrew word properly signifies, her feathers with a greenish yellow gold; which feathers in the dove are very shining, pleasant and beauteous. White, ordinarily in Scripture, denotes prosperity, felicity, triumph, glory, *etc.*, (as Judg. 5:10; Zech. 6:3, 6; Rev. 2:17, 3:4, 5, 18; and often elsewhere). And gold or golden is often used to set forth that which is flourishing, prosperous, rich, and happy. Therefore, the Babylonian monarchy is compared to the head of gold, excelling all the other, (Dan. 2:32, 38), and Babylon is called the golden one, that is, the golden city, (Isa. 14:4), and the purest and choicest oil is called golden oil, (Zech. 4:12). O! this is a very bright, sweet, and comfortable side of the text.[14]

For further clearing of this sweet lesson make note, (1) that God's afflicted shall at last escape out of their distresses into the contrary felicities. (2) Why they shall escape. (3) How God is accustomed to bring about such their escape. (4) The inferences that offer themselves hereupon.

I. That God's afflicted shall at last escape and be set free from their distress and be vested in the opposite felicities is evident,

1. By God's faithful promises to this effect in all ages. And God's promises are one sort of those two immutable things wherein it is impossible for God to lie. Take a taste of such promises in Heb. 6:13, 17, 18 and Titus 1:2.

See that God promised deliverance to Abraham's seed out of all their Egyptian afflictions. "Know of a surety, that thy seed shall be a stranger in a land that is not theirs, and shall serve them, and they shall afflict them four hundred years. And also that nation, whom they shall serve, will I judge: and

---

[14] Gen. 15:13-17; Psalm 30:5; *jubilatio* shouting joy; Isa. 54:7-8; Matt. 10:16; *cornu vel misceo,* Job 23:10; Zech. 13:9; Dan. 12:10; *Est aurum cuius color non nihil ad viretem vergit Rimchi Merc. in Pagnin Thess. ad verb.*

afterwards shall they come out with great substance...But in the fourth generation they shall come hither again," (Gen. 15:13, 14, 16).

In the days of Asaph and David, God promised to his people, "Call upon me in the day of thy trouble; I will deliver thee, and thou shalt glorify me," (Psalm 50:15).

"Because he hath set his love upon me, therefore will I deliver him: I will set him on high, because he hath known my name. He shall call upon me, and I will answer him: I will be with him in trouble, I will deliver him and honor him," (Psalm 91:14-15). How sweet also is the promise in my present text, (Psalm 68:13). In the days of Isaiah, "The Lord hath called thee as a woman forsaken and grieved in Spirit, and a wife of youth, when thou wast refused, saith thy God. For a small moment have I forsaken thee, but with great mercies will I gather thee. In a little wrath I hid my face from thee, for a moment; but with everlasting kindness will I have mercy on thee, saith the Lord thy redeemer...O thou afflicted, tossed with tempest, and not comforted, behold, I will lay thy stones with fair colors, and lay thy foundations with sapphires, and I will make thy windows of agates, and thy gates of carbuncles, and all thy borders of pleasant stones," (Isa. 54:6-8, 11-12). O! what manner of stones are here promised for the raising of this building! What manner of expressions are here to set forth this deliverance and restoration! So their escape is certain by God's faithful promises.

2. We see the people of God's frequent experiences in all generations, and their escape out of all their distresses throughout Scripture, but we read much also of their deliverances. *Many are the afflictions of the righteous; but the Lord delivers him out of them all.* God's people have many afflictions; but their God has as many deliverances for them. We read how Joseph was sold for a servant, clapped up in prison, hurt with fetters, laid in iron, *etc.*; yet, we read also how he changed his prison garments, how the king loosed him, let him go free, made him Lord of his house and ruler of all his substance, *etc.* How Israel was oppressed in Egypt and forty years afflicted in the wilderness; and yet, how at last the Lord by a mighty hand out-stretched arm brought them out of Egypt, through the wilderness, into the promised Canaan, the land of rest. How Job sat down among the ashes and scraped himself with a potsherd; and how God also turned his captivity, restoring him to double prosperity. How David was hated, persecuted, and hunted up and down by Saul from place to place, from cave to cave, from hold to hold, and yet how at last the Lord established David in peace and glory upon his royal throne. How Jeremiah was cast into the dirty dungeon, where he sank into the mire; and also how Jeremiah was lifted up again out

of the dungeon. How Jonah was thrown into the sea and devoured by the fish which God had prepared. And also, how the third day the fish cast up Jonah alive upon the dry ground. How the three Jews were bound and flung into the fiery furnace; and also how they were preserved in the furnace and delivered out of it, without having a hair of their head singed, their coats changed or the smell of fire upon them. How Daniel was cast into the den of lions; and how also Daniel was taken up again alive and without hurt, out of the lions' den. How Paul was full of afflictions in many perils—yes—sometimes pressed out of measure, above strength, *etc.*, and yet how in his abounding tribulations, he had abounding consolations by Christ, how he was delivered by the Lord out of them all—yes—sometimes from the mouth of the lion, sometimes from the jaws of death. How Lazarus lay at diverse gates, full of sores, licked by dogs, not promised the crumbs of the rich man's table (the dog's portion) so that he died; and yet how Lazarus immediately upon his death was carried by angels into Abraham's bosom. And what shall I say? We read how our dear Redeemer Jesus Christ was a man of sorrows and acquainted with grief, abasement and sufferings from his manger to his cross, endured such contradiction of sinners and at last was cruelly crucified on the cursed tree and after buried in the darksome grave; but we read also how he revived and rose again from the dead, ascended up far above all heavens leading sin, Satan, death, grave, and all our captivity captive and is sat down on the right hand of God in supreme authority, majesty, and glory; all angels, principalities, and powers—yes—all creatures being subject to him. Now all these and other experiences of the saints are most evident demonstrations that the Lord has not despised, nor abhorred the affliction of the afflicted. That verily there is a reward for the righteous; verily he is a God that judges in the earth.[15]

II. But why or when is it that God's afflicted shall one way or another at last escape out of all their afflictions and be taken from among those sullying pots and partake of the contrary mercies and felicities?

Answer: *This comes to pass:*

1. Because their God exactly knows how to deliver the godly out of temptations and tribulations, though never so intricate and perplexing. O! the infinite wisdom of God! He knows how to bring his people into troubles, when they do not know how they came there; and he knows how to bring them out of troubles, when they do not know how they came there. He knows how to do this with means and without means; by strong means, by weak means, and contrary to all

---

[15] Scripture proofs for these are Psalm 34:19, 105:17-22; Gen. 15:13-16; Exod. 1-15; Josh. 21:43-45; Job 2:7-8, 42:10; 1 Sam. 18; 2 Sam. 5:12; Jer. 38:6,13; Jonah 1:14, 2:10; Dan. 3:21-28, 6:16-23; 2 Cor. 11:23-33, 1:4-10; 2 Tim. 4:16-18; Luke 16:19-22; Isa. 53:2-4; Heb. 12:2-3; Acts 2:23; 1 Cor. 15:4; Eph. 4:8-10; Heb. 8:1; Phil. 2:7-12; Eph. 1:19-22; Psalm 22:24, 58:11.

means. So, by his angel he brought Peter (sleeping between two soldiers bound with two chains) out of prison, his chains falling off his hands and conducted him through the keepers at the prison door, through the first and second-ward, and through the iron gate of the city, which opened to them of its own accord, *etc.* Though Peter all this while did not know that it was true which was done by the angel, but then he saw a vision. So, by Cyrus and Darius he brought his captive Jews out of Babylon as strangely as if they had been fetched out of their graves. When they said, "When the Lord turned again the captivity of his people, we were like them that dream," (Psalm 116:1). This deliverance was so wonderful that it transcended their faith and almost surpassed their admiration. The Lord knows how to deliver us (us willing and unwilling, us knowing and not knowing, us waking and sleeping) out of our distresses.[16]

    2. Because their God is infinitely able and powerful to rescue his people out of their lowest ebb of tribulation. When King Darius cried to Daniel in the lions' den, "O Daniel, servant of the living God, is thy God, whom thou servest continually, able to deliver thee from the lions?" Listen to what Daniel answered, "O king live forever. My God hath sent his angel, and hath shut the lions' mouths, that they have not

---

[16] 2 Peter 2:9; Acts 12-6-12; Dan. 5:30-31, 1:1-2; *Nobis volentibus et nolentibus scientibus et nescientibus, vigilantibus et dormientibus, etc.*

hurt me," Dan. 6:20-27. As if he had said—yes, my God is able to deliver me from the lions, for he has delivered me. He that made the lions can easily shut the mouths of the lions. O! pagan king *believe* in this omnipotent God.

3. Because their God is infinitely loving, tender, and compassionate towards them in all their afflictions. So God spoke to his Zion, which dwelt with the daughter of Babylon; "He that toucheth you, toucheth the apple of mine eye," (Zech. 2:7-8). And the apple of the eye is a most tender part; the least touch, the least mote, the least hair is very painful and intolerable to it. And such was God's compassion to his afflicted Israel of old, that Isaiah says, "In all their afflictions he was afflicted and the angel of his presence saved them: in his love and in his pity he redeemed them, and he bare them, and carried them all the days of old," (Isa. 63:9); (that is, he as it were was pained in their pains, sympathizing in their sorrows; and what followed upon this?); because of his love, pity, commiserations to them; therefore, he redeemed, saved, and delivered them. Job was restored by God out of all his extremities; but why? Even because of God's love and compassions to him. "Ye have heard of the patience of Job, and ye have seen the end of the Lord," (James 5:11). That is, what a happy issue God gave of all his sufferings, and why? That, or because, the Lord is greatly compassionate in his bowels and commiserating. O! these yearning bowels and commiserations

of God were such towards afflicted Job that he would not suffer him still to lie among the ashes. How emphatically are they here expressed! That passage of Hezekiah recovered is very sweet, "Behold, for peace I had great bitterness: but thou hast in love to my soul delivered it from the pit of corruption, thou hast loved my soul from the pit of corruption," (Isa. 38:17). As if he had said, O Lord, the strength of your love, the arms of your love, the cords of you love, *etc.*, have kept me and rescued me from the grave into which I was sinking; I ascribe my life and recovery, merely to your love. O! God's dear love to his afflicted is a sweet cause of their escape out of affliction.[17]

4. Because their covenant God is ever near to and present with his people in all their deepest and darkest distresses. Therefore, they shall be supported under them and seasonably released out of all. "I will be with him in trouble, I will deliver him and honor him," (Psalm 91:15). God's presence with us in trouble is our deliverance out of trouble. He was the burning lamp in the midst of the smoking furnace, Abraham's afflicted seed, (Gen. 15:27); he was the angel in the midst of the bush (Israel) burning, but not consumed, (Exod. 3:2-6). He was with Daniel in the den of the lions, (Dan. 6:22), with the three Jews in the fiery furnace, (Dan. 3:25), with Jeremiah in the dungeon, *etc.* And therefore, they all had such

---

[17] *Ieuror signifcat commiserationem sive compassionem cum miseria alterius.* Jac. Laurent. *Com. in loc.*

safe escape. If the Lord's presence is with his people, then safety is with them, deliverance is with them, *etc*. And in due time they shall be released.

5. Finally, because their God is most faithful. The apostle gives this reason, "God is faithful, who will not suffer you to be tempted above that ye are able, but will with the temptation also make a way to escape, that ye may be able to bear it," (1 Cor. 10:13).

III. How and in what way does God take his people from the pots, deliver them from their distresses and affections?

Answer: The Lord effects and brings this about, variously and sometimes very mysteriously. As,

1. Often times by transmutations of his people's condition. How often does he literally in this life turn their darkness into light, their sorrow into joy, their sickness into health, their pain into ease, their poverty into riches, their bondage into liberty, their adversity into prosperity, their troubles into triumph, their miseries into mercies! This is as Joseph's bondage into lordship; Job's poverty into double prosperity; Hezekiah's sickness into health, *etc*.

2. Sometimes by disarming their afflictions and miseries. This is an excellent way, when the sting, venom, mischief, malignity, *etc*. of affliction is taken out and

suspended. In such case, God's people may be visibly in a state of affliction, and yet not afflicted. "As chastened, and not killed; as dying, and yet living; as sorrowful, yet always rejoicing; as having nothing, and yet possessing all things," (2 Cor. 6:9-10). Do not think it is a paradox. The bush burned, but was not consumed, (Exod. 3:2). Daniel was in the lions' den, but had no hurt by the lions, (Dan. 6:22). God disarmed the lions' paws and shut their mouths, (Dan. 3:25-27). The three Jews were in the fiery furnace, but had not a hair singed or their coats changed, nor had the smell of fire passed upon them because God suspended the burning property of the flames. So the martyr cried out of the fire, "Behold you papists that look for wonders, I feel no more pain in this fire, then in a bed of goose down, but it is to me as a bed of roses." In this way, God's dear people are sometimes without affliction, while under affliction; delivered from misery, while in misery; God disarming their afflictions of their sting, venom, and malignity.[18]

3. Sometimes, by remedying of one affliction or trouble with another. As he that by a wound was cured of an impostumation, or as physicians sometimes help a palsy or lethargy, by forcing the patient into a burning fever. So sometimes the Lord is pleased to deliver his people out of one

---

[18] *Acts and Monuments*, p. 301 vol. 2. London 1641.

affliction by another. In this way, Jonah cast overboard was saved from the sea by being devoured by the whale, (Jonah 1:15-17). He had been swallowed up, if he had not been swallowed up. He had been devoured, if he had not been devoured. The bottom of the sea had been his grave, if the belly of the fish had not been his grave. How admirable is this dispensation, when God makes one affliction an antidote against another!

4. Sometimes by elevating his people above the bitterness of their afflictions, by the surpassing sweetness of his presence and transporting consolations. Great afflictions may be on them, but greater divine refreshments may even drown and swallow them up. Our abounding afflictions are sweetly cured by Christ's abounding and super-abounding consolations, (2 Cor. 1:5). The moon and stars are in the sky at midday as well as at midnight, but not one of them then appears because the sun shining in his strength has outshined them all. So when Jesus Christ the glorious Sun of righteousness shines in his strength of grace and consolation upon the hearts of his afflicted, he so shines away their troubles and distresses that they scarce appear. If Christ sends the Spirit with faith, courage, and magnanimity and fills the heart with the consolations of God, which are not small, how easy is it to trample upon the greatest tribulation and count all afflictions as no afflictions—yes—as great advantages!

Holy Bradford the Martyr said, "I thank God more of this prison than of any parlor—yes—than of any pleasure that ever I had; for in it I find God, my most sweet good God always." And Laurence Sanders who was a martyr confessed, "I was in prison, till I got into prison." Jerome has a good note concerning Job, "That God came near to Job in his extremities, and dealt with him then most familiarly." And he adds, "Let strokes come, let all kind of punishments come so that after these Christ will come."[19]

5. Finally, if God does not release his dear people from miseries and afflictions before death, yet he always sets them at liberty by death and brings them into the contrary felicities. "Blessed are the dead that die in the Lord—they rest from their labors," (Rev. 14:13). Death cures all the saints' diseases, ceases all their pains, tears, sighs, and groans and supplies all their wants whatsoever in Christ immediately beheld and enjoyed, which is far best of all. If the Lord does not deliver us before death, he delivers us at death. And if he delivers us not from death, yet he delivers us by death. Death is our great year of jubilee, our year of release, when we shall be set at liberty from all our bondage and thralldom, from all our debts and mortgages, from all our sorrows and sufferings because from

---

[19] *Acts and Monuments*, p.308, N.50, vol. 3. London 1641; *Acts and Monuments*, p. 139, Vol. 3. London 1641; *Veniant plagae, omnia paenarum genera; dum post plagas adveniat Christus. Heronym. com. in Psalm 66. p. 93. Tom. 8 Basil 1553.*

all our sins. Oh therefore, when death approaches, then the saints may gladly lift up their heads, for their redemption draws nigh. God's people in this world are like Jonah in the tempest; this world is as the roaring and raging see, still ready to drown and swallow them up; but death, like Jonah's whale is prepared of God and swallows them up from the sea of this world so that to them there shall be no more sea. And at last this great devouring whale, death, shall be forced to cast them up again upon a safe shore of eternal rest and true felicity, at the general resurrection, that they may be where Christ is to behold his glory and live in his ravishing presence forevermore, (Phil. 1:23; 2 Cor. 5:6-9; Rev. 21:1, 20:11-13; John 17:24).

So, you see how the Lord delivers his afflicted out of afflictions.

III. Inferences here, by way of application.

Shall not God's afflicted and distressed people still lie among the pots, but at last (as with dove's wings) escape out of their deepest misery into the contrary prosperity and felicity? *Then,*

1. See here, how different is the dispensation of God's providence towards the godly and the wicked, and how different is their condition, (Psalm 68:13)? The godly must first lie here among the pots of blacking afflictions, but afterwards shall be through a happy deliverance as the wings

of a dove, covered with silver and her feathers with yellow gold; first, they are in their mourning fables, but after they are clothed with the garments of praise. First, they lie among the ashes, then after the Lord turns their captivity. First, they are in their dungeon of distresses, after they receive deliverance. First, they have their evil things and are tormented, but afterwards their good things and are comforted. But on the other hand, if you look upon the wicked, you shall find the scene is altered. They may at first be as covered with silvers, and their feathers with yellow gold; but at last they shall lie among the blackest pots of misery. First, they may flourish and spread themselves like a green bay tree, but after they shall wither like grass upon the housetops. They may now laugh, but hereafter shall have their evil things; they may now be comforted, but hereafter shall be tormented. They may first spring as the grass and flourish, but at last shall be destroyed forevermore, (Job 3:7-8, 4:10; Jer. 38:5-13; Luke 10:25; Psalm 37:30-36, 119:6-7; Luke 6:25, 16:25; Psalm 92:7).

  O! then, who would not triumph to be godly? Who would not tremble to be wicked? The godly first receive their wormwood and their gall, but afterwards their milk and honey; but contrariwise, the wicked first receive their milk and honey, and then their wormwood and their gall. O! how much better it would be to begin with gall and end with honey; to begin with sorrow and end with joy than to begin with milk and end with wormwood; than to begin with vanishing comforts and end with endless torments.

2. Therefore, let all God's afflicted people that lie among the pots of darkest sullying miseries, most patiently bear their present pressures and hopefully wait for their desired deliverance. They shall be taken from among the pots; they shall be as the wings of a dove covered with silver, *etc.*, (Psalm 68:13). Therefore, tarry for the Lord's leisure. He that believes does not make haste. The Lord's time of relaxation will come, and his time is the best time. He does all things in number, weight, and measure. There's no contradicting, diverting, or directing of him in his proceedings. He knows best when, where, and how to deliver his distressed ones. Though their sufferings are never so extreme or long, they shall at last certainly escape, either from death, or by death; either in this world, to partake sweet temporary felicity or in the world to come to enjoy sweetest everlasting glory. Therefore, patiently bear and wait a while and live by faith; the vision will not fail; at last it will speak and will not lie; and he that comes with salvation will come and will not tarry, (Hab. 2:3-4; Heb. 10-35-39).

3. Therefore, finally, this may greatly calm and quiet their spirits whose near relations lie among the pots; and also may excite their hearts to unfeigned thankfulness, whose

endeared friends are released from distress and misery to enjoy the contrary felicity.

Are you dear allies in deep afflictions, much blacked and disfigured as among the pots? You bleed in their sufferings and are exceedingly distressed upon their extremities. Yet compose yourselves—there's hope in Israel concerning this. Such as belong to God, one way or another, shall have deliverance; either from death or by death. Remember this and like promises and quiet your hearts; although you have lain among the pots, yet shall you be as the wings of a dove covered with silver, *etc.*, (Psalm 68:13; Gen. 15:13-16; Psalm 50:15, 91:14-15; Isa. 54:6-17).

Are any of your near and sweet relations released from their distresses before death or by nature dissolution? Bless God with thankfulness for his gracious dispensations. For so, God's promises are performed, God's mercies are expressed; their miseries are removed, and their felicities exalted. And, as to the present case before us touching on our dear sister deceased; though here's much matter of sadness, yet here's more matter of thankfulness. Although, it was her lot to lie a long time among the pots, in more sharp tormenting pains and miseries than many others; yet, now she has obtained a full release. And, so holy was her life, so constant her faith, so steadfast her patience to the end, and so great her interest in God, that we have no cause to doubt of her celestial felicity, or of her present triumphs in glory. It is true, our loss is great, but her gain is incomparably greater. Her husband has lost a dear, sweet, and comfortable yoke-fellow, her children have lost a tender, careful, and compassionate mother; her allies have lost a faithful, sincere-hearted friend; the poor have lost a special and liberal benefactor; the church of God has lost a holy, heavenly, and gracious saint; yes, and herself has lost something among all these losses, she has lost all her diseases, all her pains, all her sighs and groans, all her tears, all her sorrows and sufferings, all her troubles and temptations, and all her sins. But O! how much has she gained upon all these losses! She has gained heaven, glory, eternal life, the spirits of just men made perfect, the society of angels, the immediate presence and embracement of Christ, the beautifical vision and full fruition of God; the joy of her Lord and unmixed pleasures at God's right hand forevermore. These are high matters of congratulation. I say of her, to you her near relations, as sometimes Jerome said of Nepotianus to Heliodorus, "O! lament not so much that you have lost such a one, as rejoice that you have had such a one."[20] Yes, again rejoice and bless God that you have had such a one so long. Consider, her extremities on earth were intolerable, but her

---

[20] Phil. 1:21; 2 Cor. 5:1; Heb. 12:21-22; John 17:24; Phil. 1:23; Matt. 5:8; 1 John 3:2; Matt. 25:21-23; Psalm 10:11; *Nec doleas, quod talem amiteris. Sed gandeas, quod ralem habueris. Heironym. ad Heliodo Epitaph. Nepotiani. p. 23. A. Tom 1. Basil 1553.*

enjoyments in heaven are unutterable. Your losses of her may be abundantly made up in God, but what can compensate her present felicities? Her sorrow is turned into joy, her misery is swallowed up of felicity, her trouble is terminated in triumph. She has passed from the dark side to the bright side of my text. O! bless the Lord for her and rejoice with her that she lies now no longer among the pots, but is become as the wings of a dove covered with silver, and her feathers with yellow gold, (Psalm 68:13).

FINIS.

Mary Jackson the late dear and godly wife of Joseph Jackson, esq., alderman of the city of Bristol, having lived about forty years, did sweetly fall asleep in Christ, April 24, was decently interred, May 5, 1657, and is at blessed rest until Christ's second appearing, to awaken, raise, and glorify her with himself forevermore.

Reader,

There is newly published an excellent book entitled *Mysterium et Meduila Bibliorum. The Mystery and Morrow of the Bible*, that is *God's Covenants with man the first Adam before the Fall; and in the last Adam Jesus Christ after the Fall; from the beginning to the end of the world; unfolded and illustrated in positive aphorisms and their explanations.* In this, the general nature, even kinds, gradual discoveries, sanctions, and administrations of God's holy covenants, from first to last, throughout the whole Scriptures, together with their peculiar terms, occasions, author, federates, matter, form, end, properties, agreements, disagreements, and many other noted excellencies of Jesus Christ, the Soul of all covenants of faith and Mediator of the New Covenant, is described; many choice fundamental points of Christianity are explained; some practical questions or cases of conscience are resolved; adverse puzzling controversies about the present truths are positively stated and determined; many obscure and difficult Scriptures are occasionally elucidated. And, in all, the good, supernatural mystery of the whole sacred Bible, touching God's wise, gracious, merciful, righteous, plenary, wonderful, and eternal salvation of sinners by Jesus Christ through faith, sweetly couched and gradually revealed in his covenant expression in all ages of the church is disclosed and unveiled.

Francis Roberts, M.A., Pastor of the church Wrington
in the county of Sommerset.

[Roberts originally annexed this "advertisement" for his work on *Covenant* to the work on providence which you just read. It is not in print as of March, 2015. *Puritan Publications* intends on publishing this work in the future, along with Roberts' other works in separate volumes. His work on *covenant* is extremely large, almost exhaustively comprehensive and will take considerable time to publish.]

INTRODUCTION TO A BROKEN SPIRIT, GOD'S SACRIFICES

Or, The Gratefulness of a Broken Spirit to God Represented in a sermon before the right honorable House of Peers in K. Henry the Seventh's Chapel in the Abbey Westminster upon Wednesday, December 9, 1646. Being a day of public humiliation for removing of the great judgment of rain and waters then upon the kingdom.

By Francis Roberts, M.A.
Minister of Christ at Austins, London.

"Therefore also now, saith the Lord, turn ye even to me with all your heart, and with fasting, and with weeping, and with mourning; And rend your heart, and not your garments, and turn unto the Lord your God: for he is gracious and merciful, slow to anger, and of great kindness, and repenteth him of the evil," (Joel 2:12-13).

St. Augustine in soliloquy: *Inanis est poenitentia, quam sequens culpa coinquinat: nihil prosunt lamenta, si replicentur peccato: nihil valet a malis veniam possere et mala de novo iterare.*

LONDON,
Printed for *George Calvert* of *Austins Parish* in the *Old-Change* at the *sign of the Golden Fleece.*

1646.

Die Jovis 10 Decembris, 1646.

Ordered by the Lords in Parliament assembled that this house gives thanks to Mr. Roberts for his great pains taken in his sermon preached yesterday before their lordships in King Henry the Sevenths Chapel in the Westminster Abby (it being a day of public humiliation for the removing of the great judgment of rain and waters now upon the kingdom and for the preventing sad consequences on this). And he is hereby desired to print and publish the same sermon, which is to be printed only by authority under his own hand.

Jo: Browne Cler. Parliamentorum.

I appoint George Calvert of Austins Parish to print my sermon preached December 9, 1946.

Francis Roberts

A Broken Spirit

To the Right Honorable the House of Peers assembled in Parliament

Right Honorable,

The wrath of God so variously and dreadfully revealed from heaven of late against this nation, and all the ungodliness and unrighteousness of men in it, for which God's wrath has been so revealed, call and cry aloud to the entire kingdom for mature and true repentance. To making up true repentance (that holy change of the sinners person and conversation) these four necessary and eminent ingredients seem principally required, that is, (1) Conviction of sin, (John 16:8-9), (2) Contrition for sin, (Psalm 51:17; Acts 2:36-37; 2 Cor. 7:10), (3) Aversion or turning away from sin, both in inward principles and outward practices, (Isa. 1:16, 55:7; Ezek. 18:30-32), and (4) Conversion to God in Christ, both in heart and life, (Isa. 55:7, 1:17; Hos. 14:1-2; Jer. 4:1; Joel 2:12-13). For until the conscience is convinced of sin, how shall the heart be contrite for sin? Until the heart is contrite and kindly broken for sin, how shall it forsake and turn away from sin? Until the heart truly turns away from sin, how should it acceptably convert or return to God? And until the sinner returns even to God, how can he be said completely and truly to repent?

1. In conviction of sin these things seem specially implied; that is, (1) a sin-guiltiness where with the sinner may

be charged. "All have sinned," (Rom. 5:12), and Christ alone was, "holy, harmless, undefiled, and separate from sinners," (Heb. 7:26), and none could "convince him of sin," (John 8:46). (2) Clear and evident manifestation of that sin-guiltiness to the soul, by the divine light of the word and Spirit of God, (Psalm 50:21, John 3:19-20; Eph. 5:13). (3) Reflection and the turning in of the soul upon itself to take a deliberate view of sin manifested: If they shall bethink themselves; If they shall return to their heart; or "If they shall bring back to their heart," (1 Kings 8:47). (4) And finally, a self-sentencing upon this self-reflection as clearly guilty of such sin or sinfulness, (2 Sam. 12:13, Psalm 51:4, עָשָׂה {pronounced *aw-saw'*}).

    2. In contrition for sin these things seem peculiarly to be contained; that is, (1) The souls deep apprehensiveness of the hatefulness, abominableness, and sinfulness of sin wherewith it is convinced, seriously laying it to heart, as being most lively and clearly sensible of it. "My sin is ever before me," (Psalm 51:3). (2) The hearts hating, detesting, and abominating of these iniquities with indignation, so deeply apprehended, as the greatest burdens, diseases, deformities, evils, or enemies in the world, (2 Cor. 7:11). (3) The spirits inward relenting, melting, and mourning bitterly for sin in this way detested and abhorred, (Zech. 12:10-12; 2 Cor. 7:10; 2 Chron. 34:27). (4) The sinners deep debasing, humbling, loathing, and abhorring themselves for their iniquities so

abominated and lamented, (2 Chron. 33:12; Ezek. 6:9, 20:43, and 36:31; Job 42:6).

Now these inward acts of contrition oftentimes have been of old represented by outward discoveries and expressions of, (1) fasting, as counting themselves unworthy of all food, (Joel 1:14). (2) Rending of garments denotes the renting of the heart, (Joel 2:13). (3) Tears, which are as the blood of a wounded spirit, (Matt. 26; Luke 7:38). (4) Lying on the ground in self-debasement, (2 Sam. 12:16). (5) Covering their heads with ashes as counting themselves more vile than dust and ashes, (Neh. 9:1; Job 42:6; Luke 10:13). (6) Sackcloth as coarsest garments, (Esther 4:3; Jonah 3:4). (7) Striking on the thigh through inward anguish and anxiety as a travailing woman in extremity of pangs, (Jer. 31:19). (8) Beating of the breasts as deeply discontented at themselves. So the prodigal smote his breasts, (Luke 18:13).[21]

Sometimes these external expressions are without the inward acts of contrition, and then they are but as crocodile's tears, but mere hypocritical paintings. When outward expressions and inward contrition go together, they are a delectable melody even to heaven itself.

---

[21] Gerb.loc.com De Poenitent. Tom.3.c.11 paragraph 1; *Percutere semur est signum doloris, sicut mulierculae in puerperio facere solent.* Luther in Glost. marginal.

3. In aversion from sin are: (1) a new and secret antipathy in the soul against sin from an opposite principle of grace infused, (Gal. 5:17). These two are contrary one to another. (2) Ceasing to do evil both in the illicit and intemperate acts of heart and life, (Isa. 1:16), called denying ungodliness and worldly lusts, (Titus 2:11), putting away all filthiness and superfluity of naughtiness, (James 1:21), putting off the old man, (Col. 3:9), casting away of abominations as a menstrous cloth, saying to it "get you here," (Isa. 30:22). (3) Breaking off the occasions, inlets, inducements, and temptations to evil for time to come, (Psalm 119:115), as Peter fled from the high priest's hall where he was tempted, (Matt. 26). (4) Maintaining a constant intestinal combat against sin that it may be mortified, killed, and extirpated at last out of the soul, (Gal. 5:17), "the spirit lusts against the flesh," (Rom. 8:13).

4. Finally, in conversion or turning to God in Christ are considerable: (1) The motives inclining and alluring the sinner to God; that is, extreme need and misery in himself, but complete fullness and felicity in God; "How many hired servants of my father's have bread enough and to spare, and I perish with hunger?" (Luke 15:17). (2) Resolution upon those incitements to turn to God. "I will arise and go to my father," (Luke 15:18, 20). (3) Self-denying groans, desires, and cries for admittance and acceptance. "Father, I have sinned against

heaven and before you and am no more worthy to be called your son; make me as one of your hired servants," (Luke 15:18, 19). (4) Sweet closing with the God as his God in covenant; set out in these pathetic expressions, "And when he was yet a great way off, his father saw him, and had compassion, and ran, and fell on his neck, and kissed him. He said, Bring forth the best robe, and put it on him, and put a ring on his hand and shoes on his feet; and bring here the fatted calf and kill it, and let us eat and be merry," (Luke 15:20-23). O! when repentance in this way leads the poor soul into the presence of God as a Father, with what unspeakable contentment do they embrace and enjoy one another!

So, you have (right honorable) a dim portrait of some lineaments of that amiable grace of repentance. The Lord draws a perfect character of unfeigned repentance upon every one of your souls, both for your own and England's sins. Touching the second of these; that is, contrition, or brokenness of heart and the peculiar gratefulness of it to God, some plain and familiar meditations (as the narrow scantling of time allotted for preparing them would permit) have been represented in your honor's hearing and now late (with one small and necessary amplification about the opposite hardness of heart inferred) again humbly tendered to yours and the public view. May any hard-heart be softened, or any soft heart supported thereby, how my spirit should be refreshed!

God has brought two of his four sore judgments upon the land; that is, sword and pestilence; and a third of famine may overtake us except that we are aware. How highly does it concern us all, to present God daily for England's sins, with broken hearts, his well-pleasing sacrifices? Who knows how God may repent him of the evil?

To engage more fully your hearts and others in such contrition for the sins procuring these public judgments, give me leave to lay before your eyes out of the Scriptures, a list of such sins as God has been accustomed of old to threaten or punish with sword, pestilence, or famine; or with all at once: that the woe of former ages may be our warning; for all these happened to them for examples, and they are written for our admonition on whom the ends of the world are come, (1 Cor. 10:11).

I. The sword has been threatened or inflicted on people for these sins ensuing, that is:

1. Sottish ignorance of God and of his ways, (Jer. 4:19-22).

2. Disobedience to God's commands, (Deut. 25:15, 22-24; Job 36:11).

3. Backsliding from God, forsaking of God, (Jer. 15:1, 2, 6).

4. Idolatry, (Deut. 28:21-26; Judges 5:8; Psalm 78:58-63; Isa. 65:11-12; Jer. 9:13-17, 16:4, 11-12, 32:28-30, and 44:25, 27).

5. Breach of covenant, (Jer. 34:18-22).

6. Distrusting the Lord and relying on the arm of flesh, as Asa on the king of Syria, (2 Chron. 16:7-9).

7. Prophesying lies in the name of the Lord and entertaining them, (Jer. 14:13-17).

8. Mocking and misusing the messengers of God and despising God's word by them, (2 Chron. 36:15-17).

9. The sins and provocations of a profane and wicked king, as of Manasseh, (Jer. 15:2-4; 2 Kings 24:23, 41).

10. Warring against the church and people of God as Amalek did, (Exod. 17:8-16).

11. Insulting over God's afflicted church and people as Tyre did over Jerusalem, (Ezek. 26:1-15).

12. Murder, blood, cruelty, *etc.*, (2 Sam. 2:9-10).

13. Pride, haughtiness, *etc.*, (Isa. 3:16, 25).

14. Oppression, (Isa. 3:12-25; Jer. 6:4-9; Job 27:13-14).

15. Incorrigibleness under God's judgments, (Lev. 26:26-36).

II. The plague of pestilence has been threatened or inflicted on people for these offences, that is,

1. Confidence in the creature and diffidence in God, (Ezek. 33:26-27; 2 Sam. 24:2, 13, 15; Numb. 14:11-12).

2. Ungrateful murmuring against God's providence and proceedings, (Numb. 11:38, 16:41, 49).

3. Idolatry, superstition, *etc.*, (Jer. 14:10-12; Ezek. 5:11-12, 6:9-12; Numb. 25:2, 9; Josh. 22:17).

4. Condemning, opposing, or abusing God's prophets, messengers with their messages, (Jer. 29:17-20, 42:21-22).

5. Oppressing and misusing God's church and people, (Exod. 2:29; Psalm 78:50; Amos 4:10).

6. Murder and cruelty, (Ezek. 33:25, 27).

7. Adultery and wantonness, (Ezek. 33:26-27; Numb. 25:19). Of that plague there fell 24,000.

III. Famine has been threatened or inflicted upon a people for these iniquities, that is,

1. When there's no knowledge or consideration of God and his ways, (Isa. 5:12-13).

2. When a land sins against God by trespassing grievously, (Ezek. 14:13-14).

3. Carnal confidence and pride of a king in the arm of flesh, (2 Sam. 24:2, 13; 1 Chron. 21:12).

4. Idolatry, (2 Kings 18:2, 18; Jer. 13:27, 14:1-7, 16: 4, 11-12, 44:25, 27). So, Babylon's spiritual fornications shall be rewarded, (Rev. 18:3, 8).

5. Breach of covenant: as Israel's breach of covenant with the Gibeonites was plagued with diverse years of famine, though, (1) this covenant was subtly and craftily obtained. (2)

It was almost 400 years after this covenant was made that the famine was inflicted. And, (3) that breach was especially made by King Saul and his bloody house, (compare 2 Sam. 21:1-2; Josh. 9:3-17).

6. Opposing, prohibiting, and threatening of God's messengers for their messages, (Jer. 11:21-22).

7. Obstinacy and incurableness in great iniquity, (Jer. 13:22, 27; 14:1-16).

IV. Yes, all these three sore judgments, sword, pestilence, and famine are together threatened or inflicted upon people for these provocations following, that is,

1. Disobedience to God, (Jer. 42:13-18; Deut. 28:15, 21-27).

2. Carnal confidence of governors in the arm of flesh, (2 Sam. 24:2, 13; 1 Chron. 21:12).

3. Wandering from God, (Jer. 14:10-12).

4. Idolatrous abominations and wickedness, (Ezek. 5:6-7, 12:16-17, 7:4-15; Jer. 32:32-37; Ezek. 6:11-13).

5. Not harkening to God's word by his prophets and ministers, (Jer. 29:17-19).

6. Oppression, (Jer. 34:17).

7. Not being humble and contrite for sins of forefathers, (Jer. 44:9-13).

8. Incorrigibleness, when men will not be reformed—no—not by the severest judgments of God, (Lev. 26:24-26).

Thus, I have briefly indicated out of the word of God some of those sins and abominations in these several catalogues, for which the Lord has before here threatened and plagued his people with sword, pestilence, and famine (two of which this kingdom of late has sadly felt and the third is greatly feared). That your honors may clearly see the equity of God's severest proceedings with us in all this that is come upon us; and the necessity of our breaking our hearts and humbling our souls greatly in this land for all those sins and rebellions wherewith we have already pulled so much and are like to pull down more and more vengeance upon ourselves and our posterity. For which of all those abominations fore-mentioned is not England deeply guilty of? And shall England think to commit the same sins and yet escape the judgments of God?

Wherefore I most humbly and earnestly beseech your honors, that as you tender the glory of God; the true happiness of this church and state; the removing of present and preventing of future judgments; the treasuring up of blessings for the present generation and for posterity; and the re-embarking of England again in the bosom of God's favor; you would be pleased in your great zeal and wisdom to think of some way, how with the advice of the Assembly of Divines, a more full and impartial catalogue (than here has been made) of the public sins and provocations of England may be drawn up and published by authority of Parliament; and that a most solemn day of humiliation for the whole kingdom may be peculiarly set apart for afflicting of our souls deeply for those sins from Dan to Beersheba. And let the Lord accept us. Now the Father of mercies and God of all consolation, lift up your hearts in the ways of God and make you strong for all the work of God that remains upon your hand. So prays,

Your honors' faithful servant in the Lord,
Francis Roberts

THE SERMON:
A Broken Spirit, God's Sacrifices, or The Gratefulness of a Broken Spirit to God

"The sacrifices of God are a broken spirit," (Psalm 51:17).

This day we are come together to afflict our souls and mourn before the Lord because the heavens have now for diverse months together so sadly mourned upon the land in extraordinary dearth-threatening showers. These excessive showers and judgment of rain were first gendered and occasioned by the poisonous vapors of our sins and the sins of the land that have ascended and been multiplied before the Lord. One successful and approved remedy against both sin and judgment is to lay ourselves low before the Lord with penitential brokenness of spirit; and this brokenness is the peculiar subject of this text—O!—that our God would break our hearts like David's heart in its consideration.

The psalm may be justly described as David's recantation: How does he bleed and melt for his bloody sins? This sweet singer of Israel (as he is described) never prayed and sung more melodiously and pathetically than when his heart was broken most penitentially, as the birds in the spring tune most sweetly when it rains most sadly, or as some faces appear most oriently beautiful when they are most impressed with sorrow.

In this psalm are principally considerable the title and the substance of the psalm.

1. The title prefixed (which is here as the contents of a book, as the key of the psalm) contains (1) the inscription of it to the chief musician, or to the master of the music; (2) the primary or instrumental cause of it, that is, David, who ingenuously takes the shame of his sin upon his own face; (3) the occasion of the psalm, which is two-fold, that is, (i) David's iniquity, and, (ii) Nathan's ministry waking his secure conscience out of it, when the prophet came to David after he had gone into Bathsheba. The story is fully laid down in 2 Samuel chapters 11 and 12.

2. The substance of the psalm itself; in which consider: (1) the nature of kind of it, so it is a *psalmus* (εἰς τὸ τέλος ψαλμὸς τῷ Δαυιδ (Psa. 50:1)), a praying psalm; (2) its scope or end, principally to implore God's free grace and favor in the pardoning and purging of his sin and the more plenary sanctifying and comforting of his sin-afflicted heart as is evident in the current of the psalm; where it is very clear: (i) that the best of saints may *foully* fall; (ii) that the saints foully falling shall yet penitentially rise again; (iii) that when they rise after their relapses, they are embittered against their own

sins most impartially, they deal with God in their repentance most ingenuously and sincerely.[22]

3. The branches or parts of this prayer, which are chiefly two, that is, petition for himself who by murder and adultery had offered, (2 Sam. 11:1-18); and supplication for the church of God, which by his fall might be scandalized and endangered, (2 Sam. 11:18-19).

For himself, he begs restoration by arguments drawn:

1. From himself, most seriously and sincerely repenting, (2 Sam. 12:3-13).

2. From others who might be involved in like offences, whom upon such his experience of divine favor, he should be enabled feelingly to instruct in the ways of God and mysteries of conversation; then will I teach transgressors your way and sinners shall be converted to you, (Psalm 51:13). Then I that have been a patient shall become a physician to the sin-bruised souls. Then I that have had my bones so broken by my fall shall help to bind up the broken bones of others.

3. "From God's own glory," which on such beams and discoveries of grace would be tendered most illustrious, (1) "Partly in his thankful publishing of God's praises for mercies received," (Psalm 51:14-15); (2) "Partly in his dutiful sacrificing and rendering to God, not so much the carnal typical

---

[22] *Annot.* In loc.

sacrifices of the Law," (Psalm 51:15-16), which were not the things in which God did rest; "But the spiritual and true sacrifices of a broken and contrite spirit," which were the sacrifices of God's delight, in the words of the text, "The sacrifices of God are a broken spirit," (Psalm 51:17).

Having so led you to the words, let's review the treasure comprised in them; they set forth the singular gratefulness of *true broken-heartedness*. Here are two propositions emphatically discovering this: (1) affirmatively, showing in what high accounts a broken spirit is with God, the sacrifices of God are a broken spirit; (2) negatively, discovering what disrespect or unkindness of a broken heart shall never find with God—a broken and contrite heart, O! God, you will not despise. Both propositions are for substance and the same, but doubled (like Pharaoh's dream) more infallibly to assure us of the certainty of it; and therefore, in the handling of the first proposition we shall in effect have the sense of both.

In the affirmative proposition you have first the subject—a broken spirit. Secondly, the predicate affirmed of this subject, that it is the sacrifices of God. The copula knitting both together is not expressed in the Hebrew text, but must necessarily be supplied to make up the sense perfect (*is* or *are*); therefore, here the word 'are' is put in a different character.

Now, for clearing the sense of this proposition these things are a little to be opened; that is,

1. What is here meant by the word 'spirit'? 2. What is intended by a broken spirit? 3. In what sense we are to understand that such a broken spirit *is* the sacrifices of God.

First, by the word 'spirit' [רוּחַ *ruwach*] the Scripture is accustomed to point out to us several things: If any word in the Old or New Testament is of multifarious signification, certainly this word 'spirit' is one. But as to this place, by spirit understand—first, not the regenerate part in a child of God, in whom 'spirit' stands opposed to 'flesh,' or grace to sin. "The spirit lusteth against the flesh and the flesh lusteth against the spirit," (Gal. 5:17); see also John 3:6. For in this place brokenness and contrition is rather a spark of that regenerate part, and part of the new man, subjectively inherent and seated in the spirit here spoken of, as its receptacle. Secondly, nor the intellective part, as distinct from the sensitive and from the corporeal part of man; as the apostle makes the distribution; "that your whole spirit and soul and body are preserved blameless," (1 Thess. 5:23). As Calvin, Beza, and others observe which spirit is elsewhere styled the spirit of the mind. For though the intellective part, as some of the schoolmen think, are the more special subject of this brokenness, yet cannot the sensitive appetite be secluded—

yes—the body itself cannot but sympathize and become broken when the heart and sprit are broken. Thirdly, but here understand the heart or soul of man principally, which is the most proper receptive subject of this penitential brokenness.[23]

Secondly, by a *broken spirit*, so conceive in general; it is a metaphor from corporal things, as from an earthen vessel, a tree, the bones or body of a man, or the like, which are properly liable to be broken, and (that I may here allude to the Hebrew word used) shivered to pieces: The spirit cannot be said to be broken properly, but allusively, metaphorically, when for sin, *etc.*, it is humbled, as in Manasseh, (2 Chron. 33:12). It is pricked and wounded as in Peter's hearers, (Acts 2:37); it is softened and melted as in Josiah, (2 Chron. 34:27); it is in bitterness, as in those intended, (Zech. 12:10-11).[24]

---

[23] *Quod autem sequitur, ita explico cum doctissimo interprete, ut quod in genere dictum erat, per partes explicetur. Mentem igitur Paulus Spiritus appellatione significat, illud nempe in quo nativa praecipua labes inest, Animam vero reliquas inferiotes facultates, non quasi duae sint animae, sed quod suo more Paulus functiones unius ejuideoque animae distribuat, cujus etiam alicubi tres facultates cotnmemorat, ut diximus, (Eph. 4:17). Corporis denique nomine satis constat animae domicilium significari. Beza in loc. Estuis in Distinctionem 16. lib. 4.*

[24] *Radix proprie significat, fregit, sicut si anguntur ligna Exod. 9:26; Off. Exod. 12:46. Vasa testacea Lev. 6:28. Statuae 2 Kings 11:19. LXX plenumque redd derunt per oppiossone seu depressione contuses est humilis spiritu, etc. Ex quibus omnibus patet, contritionis nomine meraphorice micilgi si actionem et scissionem cordis, verum acserium dolorem, quo vis et robur cordis veluti conteritui, sicut per morbos robui corporis. Quidam metaphoram desumptam esse dicunt a vase testaceo quod in minitussima fracta redigitur, (Psalm 31:13; Isa. 30:11; Jer. 19:11). Alij ab offibus quae subito lapsu in plura fragmenta dissilrunt, ut bestiatum dentibus assulatim*

More particularly here, understand by brokenness of spirit, *the following:*

1. Not a mere natural brokenness and tenderness, which arises from the tender temper and construction of the heart and eyes by nature, which is in some more, some less; when they are ready to receive impressions of grief and to make expressions in tears, upon occasion of any pathetical objects. This being but a fruit of nature cannot be the spiritual sacrifices of God, acceptable to him.

2. Not a mere worldly brokenness and grief of heart, arising from some worldly ground or occasion, *etc.* Such as Jacob's grief for Joseph supposed to be torn in pieces, (Gen. 37:33-35), of David for Absalom, (2 Sam. 18:33), of Rachel for her children, (Matt. 2:18), as streams of water will not ascend higher than the fountainhead when they first took their rise, so these streams of worldly contrition, arising merely from a worldly principle can never ascend higher than the world; and in sin the sorrow of the world works death, (2 Cor. 7:10).

3. Not any formal feigned hypocritical brokenness for sin, which comes near to true penitential brokenness and is the liveliest shadow or picture of it, but no more; whereby a man may be first convinced mightily of his sin committed; secondly, wounded and afflicted in conscience deeply upon

---

comminuantur, (Psalm 38:33; Isa. 38:13; Osc. 6:5; Gerbard in loc. com. Tom. III. De Panitent.c.II. sect 1.)

such conviction; thirdly, even forced voluntarily to confess the sin publicly before others for which he is perplexed; fourthly, brought to make some outward satisfaction by restitution of dishonest gain; fifthly, and at last through extremity of anguish and horror of conscience is so swallowed up of utter despair, as to make away himself. All these were found in Judas, who yet *never found* a true brokenness of spirit, (Matt. 27:3-5). But the God of truth delights only in truth and sincerity, and abhors hypocrisy.[25]

4. But here understand only a true, gracious, penitential brokenness of heart for sin, when the heart is kindly pricked, melted, humbled, and in bitterness for sin and finding no rest nor remedy in itself, nor in any created comfort, makes out only to God's favor in Jesus Christ for support and ease. This is a proper fruit of that sweet spirit of grace promised, (Zech. 12:10-12). This is that "godly sorrow that worketh repentance not to be repented of," (2 Cor. 7:10). This is for substance that, "repentance to life," (Acts 11:18), or an eminent branch of it. And this was the brokenness of spirit

---

[25] In this way one discriminates between the elect and reprobate in this point. *Eliciti ex sensu peccato, iraeque dei apprehensione spiritus sancti ductus, volentes consugiunt ad deum, ut in Davide, Jobu, aliisque videre est. Reprobi vero ut Cain compunct desperant, dicentes major est iniquit as nostra, quam ut sustinere possumus; aut hyopocritae sese prosternunt ut Achab, aut desperabundi sibi mortem consciscunt, ut Achitophel, Judas, Nero, Diocletianus, Christanorum persecutotes atrocissimi; vel intus contreniscunt ut Caligula aut toto corpore concutiuntur nullum petentes remedium, ut Baltassar, qui viso digito in pariete scribente ita fuit consternates, ut concussis genibus vacillaret. Juan. Malculmi Comment in Acts 1:37.*

which was upon David in penning this psalm, which he declares to be the acceptable, "sacrifices of God," (Psalm 51:17).

This brokenness of spirit in a child of God may be considered either *as it is:*

1. Habitual; that is, the habit of brokenness, tenderness, *etc.*, which is infused into the heart of the regenerate at first conversion, which is called in the New Covenant, "a heart of flesh," (Ezek. 11:19, 36:26). The heart of stone noting that habitual hardness that is in carnal men. The heart of flesh that habitual softness and brokenness that is in spiritual men.

2. As it is actual; that is, that exercise of brokenness and tenderness of heart for sin upon just occasions, as David reduced his brokenness into action upon his fall, *etc.* That is a brokenness impressed on us, this a brokenness expressed by us.

3. In what sense is such a broken spirit here described the sacrifices of God?

Answer: This phrase *the sacrifices of God* may bear a doubled interpretation; that is, either first as denoting the singular excellency of this sacrifice of a broken heart. It is usual in the Hebrew tongue to add the name of God to a thing, so set out the excellency of it, as the mountains of God, *i.e.,* exceeding high mountains, (Psalm 36:6); cedars of God, most tall cedars, (Psalm 80:11); rivers of God, (Psalm 65:10); wrestlings of God, *i.e.*, great wrestlings, (Gen. 30:8); harps of God, (Rev. 15:2), so here sacrifices of God, *i.e.*, most choice, excellent sacrifices. Or secondly, as signifying the peculiar gratefulness and singular acceptableness of this sacrifice to God, above all the typical sacrifices of the law, none of them all please God as well as the broken and contrite spirit; this to God is the sacrifice of sacrifices. Now this latter seems to be most clearly here intended.

1. Partly because a broken heart is here opposed to all ceremonial sacrifices, (Psalm 51:16-17). These God neither desires nor delights in, in comparison of a broken heart and spirit.

2. Partly because this broken heart is here called emphatically not only the sacrifice of God in the singular number, but the sacrifices of God in the plural, to note that this one sacrifice of a truly broken heart has in it the gratefulness of all sacrifices. With this one, God is better pleased than with all others fore-mentioned.[26]

---

[26] *Sacrificia dei postquam sacrificiis destraxit propitiandi Dei virtutem, quam falso affinxerant Judaei, nunc dicit, Etiamsi nihil praeter Cor contritum et humiliatum afterat, hoc Deo abudne sufficere; quia unum hoc exigat a peccatoribu ut de jecti et prostrate, misericord am implorent; neque frustra plurali numero ulius est, quo melius exprimeret poenitentiae Sacrilicium, pro omnibus unum sufficere. Si dixisse honi odoris esse hoc Sacrificii genus promptum fuisset Judaeis cavillari, alias tamen esse species quae*

3. Partly because it is said by way of exegetical amplification in the latter part of this verse, *a broken and contrite heart, O God, you will not despise*, which being spoken was intended; you will not despise, *i.e.*, you will highly esteem and account of it; it will be most acceptable with you. The words in this way explained, this doctrinal proposition is evident in them. *That is, a truly broken spirit is a most pleasing and acceptable sacrifice to God.*

A broken spirit is not only grateful to the saints themselves, refreshing both their souls and the souls of others, as a seasonable April shower does the grass; nor only delightful to the very angels of heaven: "There is joy in the presence of the angels of God, over one sinner that repents, more than over ninety-nine just persons that need no repentance," (Luke 15:7-10). Upon which says Bernard, *Delicia Angelorum sunt lacryma poenitentium*, the tears of penitents are the delights of angels. But (which is most of all) a broken spirit is the delight of God himself, his most grateful sacrifice. This may be evidenced chiefly in two ways: (1) on *that* it is so, and (2) *why* it is so.

---

non minus deo placeient. Sicut videmus hodie Papistas, sua opera dei graciae miscere, negratuita sit peccatorum remissio; Consulto itaque David ut omnia satisfactionum commenta excluderer unicum spiritus dejectionem, quaecunque oblique modere hypocritas, qui suo tantum arbitrio Sacrificia estumant, dum ad propitiandum deum valere arbitrantur. Calvin in Psalm 51:17.

1. For the first, the 'O! that this is so'; that is, that a truly broken spirit is a most pleasing sacrifice to God may be cleared on many considerations.

1. A broken spirit is so pleasing to God that he prefers this one alone to all ceremonial sacrifices and external rites under the Old Testament whatsoever, "For thou desirest not sacrifice, else would I give it: thou delightest not in burnt-offering. The sacrifices of God are a broken spirit," (Psalm 51:16-17). There were many sacrifices under the Old Testament: the burnt-offering, the sin-offering, the meat-offering, the drink-offering, the daily sacrifice, *etc*. And these sacrifices were not only prescribed of God, but also in their kind and season accepted also of him, (2 Sam. 24:25; 1 Kings 18:36-38). Notwithstanding, God looked more at a *penitential broken heart* than at all those. Therefore, he says elsewhere, "Rend your hearts and not your garments," (Joel 2:13). And no wonder; for (1) these were but outward sacrifices; this of a broken spirit is inward; (2) those were of dead creatures, dead beasts, *etc.* this is of living men; (3) those were typical, this was real; (4) those would be of acceptance with God, but for a season, until the incarnation of Christ, (Heb. 10:5-9); this will

be grateful to God forever, both under the Old and New Testaments.[27]

2. A broken spirit is so pleasing to God that God highly prefers it before all mere mortal performances or pharisaical perfections whatsoever; this is conspicuous in that eminent parable of the Pharisee and publican, (Luke 18:10-15). Here we find some remarkable thoughts, (1) The devotion they perforated; they both went into the temple to pray. (2) The manner of their performance; the Pharisee was upon tiptoes with God, negatively disclaiming a manifold guiltiness; *God I thank you that I am not as other men are—extortioners, etc.*; he borrows God's name, pretending to thank him, intending to praise and applaud himself. Affirmatively, assuming to himself a manifold virtuousness—*I fast twice in a week, etc.* But the poor publican performs his devotion in a far other manner—he stood a far off—as afraid to draw near into the presence of God; he would not so much as lift up his eyes to heaven, as unworthy to look towards God's glorious habitation; he smote upon his breast, as sore broken and displeased at himself for his own offences; and said, *God be merciful to me a sinner*, as apprehending no sufficient remedy,

---

[27] *Holocaustis non delectabetis. Nihil ergo offeremus? Sic veniemus ad deum? Unde illum placabimus? Often sane in te habes quod citeras. Noli extrinsecus thara comparere; sed dic in me sunt dues votatua, quae reddun laudes tibi. Noli extrinsecus pecus quod mactes inquirere, habes in te quod occidas. Sacrificium, etc.* Augustine *enarrat in Psalm 50.*

against his deep sinful misery, but only divine mercy. In this way the Pharisee wholly exalted himself, the publican wholly debased himself. The Pharisee only praised himself, the publican only dispraised himself; the Pharisee only justified himself, the publican condemned himself. (4) But in closing this, see the testimony of Christ touching their acceptance: *I tell you this man went down to his house justified rather than the other*, i.e. justified and not the other. O! how happy are they that partake of God's justification, (Psalm 32:1-2). To be justified of God is a fruit of his highest acceptation. This acceptation was the privilege of the broken-hearted publican, when the cracking Pharisee with all his moral and legal perfections without true contrition was rejected.[28]

3. A broken spirit is so pleasing to God that God has a peculiar and especial respect thereunto. "Thus saith the Lord, The heaven is my throne, and the earth is my footstool, where is the house that ye build to me? And where is the place of my rest? For, all those things hath my hand made, and all those things have been saith the Lord; but to this man will I look, even to him that is poor and of a contrite spirit," (Isa. 66:1-2). God looks upon him that is of a poor and contrite spirit, not only with a look of bare intuition, for so he looks upon both

---

[28] *Impropria comparatio: neq; enim quasi communis ambobus sit justitia,* Publicanum Christus tantum gradu aliquot prefert; sed intelligit eum gratum; suisse deo, quum Pharisaeus in totum rejectus fuerit. Calvin *in loc.*

the evil and the good; but with a "look of smiling favor and acceptation," called the, "lifting up of the light of his countenance," (Psalm 4:6), now where God thus looks, he likes, he notably loves. So it's said, "God had respect to Abel and to his offering," (Gen. 4:4). God approved it, accepted it, and was well-pleased with it. So God respects and accepts a broken-heart. How great respect had God to Josiah and his brokenness of heart, saying, "Because thine heart was tender, and thou didst humble thyself before God, when thou heardest his words against this place, and against the inhabitants thereof, and humblest thyself before me, and did rend thy clothes, and weep before me, I have even heard thee also saith the Lord," (2 Chron. 34:27-28). How great respect had God to King Manasseh (that monster of wickedness) and to the brokenness of his spirit, for, "when he was in affliction, he besought the Lord his God, and humbled himself greatly before the God of his fathers: And prayed unto him, and he was entreated of him, and heard his supplication, and brought him again to Jerusalem into his kingdom," (2 Chron. 33:12-13). In a word what respect Christ had to the penitent woman's brokenness of spirit, when he so commends her entertainment of himself with tears, washing of his feet with them, wiping them with the hairs of her head, *etc.*, before the Pharisees entertaining of him with all his dainties and complements, "to the end," (Luke 7:36). Now all this respect which God so peculiarly manifests to brokenness of spirit makes it clear that a broken spirit is God's most grateful sacrifice and delight. (Or, [בָּזָה bazah {baw-zaw'}]. He submitted himself exceedingly.)

4. A broken spirit is so pleasing to God that he ranks a broken spirit, a tender, fleshy heart, a spirit of mourning, *etc.*, among the rarest expressions of his special grace and favor promised to his church. Therefore, where God promises to be to his people, "a little sanctuary in the countries where they shall come—their gathering again—the reformation of the land—oneness of the heart—newness of spirit," *etc.*, he adds, "And I will take the stony heart out of their flesh and will give them a heart of flesh," (Ezek. 11:16-21). And elsewhere, after other promises God says, "Then will I sprinkle clean water upon you, and you shall be clean, from all your filthiness and from all your idols will I cleanse you. A new heart also will I give you, and a new spirit will I put within you, and I will take away the stony heart out of your flesh, and I will give you a heart of flesh," (Ezek. 36:24-26); yes, when those evangelical blessings are promised to the "house of David and inhabitants of Jerusalem, the spirit of grace and of supplication"; it is added, "And they shall look upon me whom they have pierced, and they shall mourn for him, as one mourneth for his only son, and shall be in bitterness for him as one that is in

bitterness for his firstborn," (Zech. 12:10). Where brokenness of spirit for the sins that broke and pierced Christ is expressed under the notions, of mourning as for an only son, of being in bitterness as for a firstborn, of great mourning as of Hadadrimmon in the valley of Megiddo, where good Josiah was slain. Now why should this brokenness of spirit be ranked in this way among God's choice promised blessings, if the Lord did not have choice thoughts and account of it?

5. A broken spirit is so grateful to God that he undertakes it to be the peculiar physician to heal, bind up, revive, and comfort poor broken hearts and bleeding souls. He heals the broken in heart and binds up their wounds, (Psalm 147:3). He bottles up their tears and their sighing is not hid from him. He dwells in the "high and holy place, with him also that is of a contrite and humble spirit; *but to what end?* To revive the spirit of the humble and, to revive the heart of the contrite ones," (Isa. 57:15). Grief and sorrow kills, but joy and comfort revive. It's true, God sometimes sets off the beauty of his own sweet comforts by the darksome shadow of trouble of spirit and broken bones inflicted upon us; he casts down that he may lift us up; he crushes that he may consulate us; yes, he kills us that he may more gratefully revive us; as one said.[29]

---

[29] *Dejicit, ut relevet: permit, ut solatia praestet: Enecat, ut posit vivificare Deus.*

Still the scope and intendment of God is the swathing up of broken bones, the sweetening of the embittered spirits of his people. This is the very office of Jesus Christ himself, "The Lord hath anointed me to preach good tidings to the meek, he has sent me to bind up the broken-hearted—to comfort all that mourn. To appoint unto them that mourn in Zion, to give unto them beauty for ashes, the oil of joy for mourning, the garment of praise for the spirit of heaviness," (Isa. 1:1-3); compare this with Luke 4:18. These are happy tears which Christ's hand shall wipe off; happy wounds which Christ's blood shall close again; happy brokenness of heart, which Christ shall bind up, *etc.*, behold how God, how Christ, loves a broken heart.[30]

6. Finally, a true broken spirit is so acceptable to God that he is pleased to select and single out the broken heart, the poor and contrite spirit, for his peculiar habitation and for the place of his rest. "Where is the place of my rest?" says God. He answers that, "to this man will I look, even to him that is poor and of a contrite spirit," as if he should say that here is my rest, here will I place my eye and heart, here will I repose myself and dwell, (Isa. 66:1-2). But more clearly, "Thus saith the high and lofty one that inhabiteth eternity, whose name is

---

[30] *Felices lachrymae, quas benigne manus conditoris abitergunt; et beati culiqui in talibusliquesie ielegerunt, quam elevaum superbum, qui omne sublime videre, quam avaritiae et petulantiae timulati.* Bernard *de contemp. mundi.*

holy, I dwell in the high and holy place, with him also that is of a contrite and humble spirit," (Isa. 57:15). God will not dwell with the proud, hard, impenitent, and unbelieving heart, yet will dwell with the contrite and humble spirit. What? God dwells there? How dear is such a heart to God? It is not said that saints or angels shall dwell with such, though they are sweet companions; not peace, joy, comfort, life, grace, holiness, happiness; *etc.*, shall dwell there, though these are dear delights able to change the blackest midnight into a smiling morning, a very prison into a palace and the vale of the shadow of death into a mountain of life and joy. But it is said that the high and lofty One that inhabits eternity, *will* dwell with him that's of a humble and contrite spirit. O! how does the highest God descend; how does the lowest heart ascend in such an inhabitation! The broken heart says with the centurion, "Lord, I am not worthy that you should come under my roof; much less that you should dwell there."

II. Thus much of the *broken spirit* that it is a most pleasing sacrifice to God. Now we pass to the second particular.[31] Why should a truly broken spirit be so *grateful* to the sacrifices to God? This may be opened both negatively and affirmatively.

---

[31] θυσία τῷ θεῷ πνεῦμα συντετριμμένον καρδίαν συντετριμμένην καὶ τεταπεινωμένην ὁ θεὸς οὐκ ἐξουθενώσει (Psa. 50:19).

Negatively, this *gratefulness* of a broken spirit, does not arise from any merit, or any degree or shadow of merit that may be imagined to be, (1) In a broken spirit (as the popish merit-mongers do commonly suggest when they treat of this theme of brokenness of heart). For though our, "heads were waters, and our eyes fountains of tears," (Jer. 9:1). Though we should, "eat ashes as bread, and mingle our drink with weeping," (Psalm 102:9), though, "all the night long we should make our bed to swim, and water our couch with tears," (Psalm 6), that our eyes were dim with grief, our cheeks furrowed with sorrow and, "our very moisture turned into the droughts of summer," (Psalm 32:4); yet when all is done, we are but unprofitable servants, what have we done more than duty? No, for ground, manner, and end of all our penitential mournings for sin, so do we not come short of duty? Alas, for us, *ipsae lachrymae sunt lacrymabiles*, we had need to weep over our tears, sigh over our sobs, mourn over our griefs, be broken for our brokenness and to repent over our very repentance; not that these duties are performed by us, but that they are performed no better when we have done our best, for so much flesh adheres to everything we do. We read of David's broken bones, but we do not read of his merit; we read of Peter's bitter tears for his sin, but we do not read a word of their satisfaction that must be left forever to the blood of Christ.[32]

Affirmatively, a broken spirit is a most grateful sacrifice to God *because:*

1. A broken spirit is a spiritual sacrifice. In this, not the bodies or blood of dead, brute beasts, but the spirit itself of a living and reasonable man, even his very heart and soul, is sacrificed to God (and the spirit of one is better than all the beasts and earthly creatures in the whole world); and the spirit of man offered is not his spirit as stone and carnal, but as broken and spiritual with godly sorrow and repentance? The spirit is the best of man; a broken spirit is the best of spirits.

Now God insists much on the spiritual nature of his sacrifices and service, so he specially calls for the heart, "My son give me thine heart," (Prov. 23:26); all the gospel sacrifices, which are acceptable to God in Christ, they are, "spiritual sacrifices," (1 Peter 2:5), living sacrifices, "I beseech you therefore brethren, by the mercies of God, that ye present your bodies a living sacrifice, holy, acceptable to God, which

---

[32] *Quod contritionem attinei, nos eam in poenitentia vera necessariam statuimus modo et dolorem illum ob peccato secundum Deum intelligamus, et pro peccatis satisfactorium non agnoleamus; Gratiae enim Dei, non contritioni attribuenda est peccatorum remission. Ut glossa de poenitnent distinct. 201 contra concil Tridenum definionem Sess. 14.c.4. recte exposait. Synopsipur Theol Disp 32 lacrymas ejus lego, satisfactionem non lego.* Petri Serm. 46.c.46 Augustine Serm. 117 de Temp.

is your reasonable service, or, your service according to the word," (Rom. 12:1). God himself is, "a spirit, and will be worshipped in spirit," (John 4:24), and the more the spirit of man is spiritual, the more it becomes like God.

2. A broken spirit is a true and sincere spirit. It does not hypocritically, "cover its sin like Adam," (Job 31:33), or spare any iniquity as Saul did Agag, *etc.* But like a broken vessel, lets all run out, ingenuously spreads open all its own vileness before the Lord, takes the shame of all upon its own face, let us all lie loose; as water, mire, stones, heterogeneous, which were inseparably congealed in a hard bound frost, yet they all lie loose when there comes a kindly thaw; so the heart that was once congealed in the mire and dregs of sin, when the penitential brokenness is kindly thawed and dissolved, sins that stuck fastest in the soul lie loose, the spirit longs to be rid of them all, as here broken-spirited David lamented both originals and actuals. He does not spare even his foulest and shameful miscarriages, and prays they would be, "thoroughly purged" from all, (Psalm 51:27). So Paul, after he became a man of a broken spirit, freely rips up his foulest enormities, confesses he was a, "blasphemer, and a persecutor, and injurious," (1 Tim. 1:13), elsewhere he says, "I verily thought with myself that I ought to do many things contrary to the name of Jesus of Nazareth. Which thing I also did in Jerusalem, and many of the saints did I shut up in prison,

having receive authority from the chief priests, and when they were put to death I gave my voice against them, and I punished them often in every synagogue, and compelled them to blaspheme, and being exceedingly mad against them, I persecuted them even unto strange cities," (Acts 26:9-11). And it is observable how God's promise of a "heart of flesh" is coupled with the promise of "sprinkling clean water" upon people of, "cleansing them from all their filthiness and from all their uncleanness," (Ezek. 36:25-29). A heart of flesh and uncleanness cannot peaceably lodge together; it would sincerely abandon all and its bitterness for all and take pleasure in that bitterness; counterfeits are a trouble in sin like the Pharisees with their sour, "disfigured faces," (Matt. 6), and does not squeeze out a few crocodile tears, but his very soul bleeds and his eye trickles down with tears in secret, powering out complaints into the bosom of God, when no eye but his sees. *Ille dolet vere, qui sine teste dolet.*[33]

Now God calls for uprightness, "walk before me and be thou upright," (Gen. 17:1); he loves sincerity and "Truth in the inward parts," (Psalm 51:6), and Nathaniel is prized and commended of Christ for a "True Israelite indeed," because in him "there was no guile," (John 1:27).

---

[33] *Verus poenitens de peccatis dolet, et de dolore gaudet. Synops. Par. Theol. Disp. 32 paragraph 35.*

3. A broken spirit is a gracious spirit. It's part of the grace promised in the current of the New Covenant, (Ezek. 11:19, 36:26-27); its one fruit and that a principal one of the "spirit of grace" promised, (Zech. 12:10). Consequently, its part of that precious image of God consisting in true holiness (Eph. 4:24), and, a rich link of that admirable chain of grace about the church's neck, (Song of Solomon 4:9). (So Junius and Ainsworth expound this expression *vid atrumq in loc.*)

And therefore, God is taken much with a truly broken heart. He cannot choose but to accept and prize his own. Graces in us love his own image and the reflexive rays of his own beauty upon his. Christ pathetically professes to his church as much, "Thou hast ravished heart, my sister, my spouse; thou hast ravished my heart with one of thine eyes, with one chain of thy neck; the smell of thine ointments is better than all spices—the smell of thy garments is like the smell of Lebanon," (Song of Solomon 4:9-11).

4. A truly broken spirit is also a believing spirit. Faith and repentance are inseparable twins bred together in one and the same sanctified womb of the converted soul. Faith first is in us in order of nature at least, but actual repentance is apt first to appear; as sap and life are first in the root, yet buds leaves and fruit first discover themselves in the branches. They shall look upon Him whom they have pierced. There's faith, for with what other eye can they behold Christ

crucified? "And they shall mourn for him;" there's brokenness of spirit resulting from it, (Zech. 12:10). There is a hard question in divinity—whether faith is not part of repentance? In this, some resolve, if repentance is considered largely for the whole work of conversion, so faith is comprised in it; if strictly, so it is the cause thereof; however, they are nearly allied sister-graces.

Now faith wonderfully "pleases God," (Heb. 11:5-6), so we read of such a catalogue of faith's triumphs and glorious achievements in that chapter. Faith most highly honors God and God highly honors faith. Faith clasps fast hold of Jesus Christ, as its peculiar object and comes into the presence of God with Christ crucified in its arms, urges his person and passion, as sin's propitiation; counts all self-righteousness "loss and dung" in comparison of Christ's righteousness, (Phil. 3:7-8). This is that which so singularly pleases God in as much as the person of Christ is most dear to God, his "beloved Son," (Matt. 3:17), the "Son of his love," (Col. 1:13), his "only begotten Son," (John 3:16), "in whom he is well pleased," (Matt. 3:17); yes, in whom "his soul delighteth," (Isa. 42:1), and the passion of Christ is "an odor of a sweet smell to God, (Eph. 5:2-3), no pillar of most fragrant incense or perfume is any way comparable to it. In this way, brokenness of spirit entwined with faith and faith fast linking itself to Christ becomes most grateful to God.

5. Finally, a broken spirit is a self-debasing spirit. Such a spirit can lay itself low before God as vile in its own eyes. See this in several people; the Pharisee and the publican, both of them went up to the temple to pray, but they went about the same work with far different hearts. The Pharisee was stony and unbroken; therefore, he only exalts himself, cracks and brags of himself, and justifies himself before all others. The publican's heart was fleshy and broken; and therefore, vilifies himself, dejects, debases, and abhors himself, (Luke 18:10-15). See this in the self-same persons, comparing them with themselves being found in several states and conditions. Paul, before he was broken in heart, "was alive," (Rom. 7:9), and stood much upon his native or acquired privileges, (Phil. 3:2-3), but when once he kindly broke, he confesses all these things to be loss—yes—loss *and dung*, and counts himself unworthy to be called an apostle, (1 Cor. 15:9), less than the least of all saints, (Eph. 3:8), chief of sinners, (1 Tim. 1:15); now he vales all of his topsails and sits down in the dust. So, the prodigal, when his spirit became broken, debases himself exceedingly, "Father, I have sinned against heaven and before thee, and am no more worthy to be called thy son, make me as one of thine hired servants," (Luke 15:18-19), as if he had said any, even the meanest of all relations to his father, is far too good for him. So, the sinful woman, when her heart was penitentially broken for sin, debases herself; she addresses

herself not to Christ's head, but to his very feet and there she falls weeping and with her tears she washes, with part of her head she wipes, with her mouth she kisses, and with her costly ointment she anoints his very feet; she thought it was an honor enough for her. She was exceedingly happy that she might have liberty to perform the very meanest and lowest services to Christ, (Luke 7:38). O! a heart thoroughly broken for sin is greatly out of conceit with itself, can lie down in the dust at the foot of God, can be as anything, and can be as nothing that God in Christ may be all.[34]

Now the Lord greatly prizes a self-despising spirit, has respect to such, (Isa. 66:1-2), and, "will dwell with such to revive them," (Isa. 57:15). And how was the self-debasing publican justified before the Pharisee? (Luke 18). How was the self-debasing prodigal entertained of his father, (Luke 15:14)? Yes, how was the self-debasing penitentiary commended and comforted by Christ? (Luke 7:44-46) Who from this principle of broken heartedness was so mean and vile in their own apprehensions.

So we have seen the doctrinal handling of this observation; now to the *practical* application. Is a truly broken spirit such grateful sacrifices of God? Then how useful is this

---

[34] *Summum est hoc Sacrificium aliis omnibus praeferri a deo, dum fidels vera sui abnegationesie prostrate jacent, ut nihil de se altum sapiant, sed patianturse in nihilum redigi.* Calvin *in Isaiah 66:2.*

doctrine, both to teach, to try, to exhort, and to comfort us about this mystery of a broken heart.

This may teach and inform us, chiefly about these two things:

1. That there is a vast odds and disparity between that account which God, and that which the world has, of a broken spirit. With God a broken and a contrite spirit (as has been showed) is most acceptable, beyond all typical sacrifices, before all mere mortal performances and pharisaical perfections, peculiarly respected of God, ranked among the choice and flowered of promised blessings, the special cure of God, and the very home and habitation of the Lord himself most high and holy. But on the contrary, this brokenness of heart is with the world, and the men of the world most unacceptable, is looked upon as a said, mopish, melancholy, and disconsolate distemper; always contrary to their genius, who resolve to crown themselves with rosebuds, before they are withered and to let no flower of the spring overpass them; who say with the rich fool, "Soul thou hast much goods laid up for many years, eat, drink, and by merry," (Luke 12:19). However, the saints know the world is grossly mistaken in this matter of brokenness of the spirit for sin and while God himself counts in his sacrifice, they can say it is a wholesome

brokenness, a sweet bitterness, a joyful sorrow, and happy tears.[35]

2. That an unbroken spirit, a hard-flinty adamantine heart is on the contrary most hateful and abominable to God. A broken and contrite heart he cannot despise; an unbroken heart consequently he cannot but despise. Take a short view of (1) the nature of a hard heart, and (2) of the odiousness of such a heart to God.

The nature of a hard heart (which Scripture sometimes calls a heart waxing gross, or fat, and so senseless, (Acts 28:27), and often elsewhere, a stony heart, (Ezek. 11:19, 36:26), hardness of heart, (Mark 3:5), and hardness, (Rom. 2:5) may be considered as it is hardened (1) naturally, (2) actually and accidentally, (3) habitually, and (4) judicially.

1. Naturally every man's heart is a hard heart; a very stone, for intractableness and obduration. This is evident by the tenor of the Covenant of Grace, in which God first undertakes to removes the stony heart, before he gives a fleshly heart, (Ezek. 11:19, 36:26-27); therefore, until God by supernatural dispensation bestow a tender heart, everyone by nature lies under the curse of a hard heart. And this natural hardness of heart is compared, not to the hardness of wax,

---

[35] *Oemitus dictus quasi geminatus luctus, quem merito fideles appetunt, quoniam diligentes consolatur, poenitentes emundat, diabolum effugat, Christo conciliate, amaritudo dulcis, Lachrymae felices, salutaras afflictio.* Cassindor. Tur. Psalm.

brass, iron, or steel (for though these are very hard, yet they become soft and malleable by the fire), but to the hardness of a very stone, which will be sooner broken to powder than softened, as Zanchy observes, so extreme is our natural hardness.[36]

2. Actually and accidentally, not only the hearts of natural men, but also even of regenerate person may contract some hardness, spiritual security and stupidity; by not improving grace received, and other means for maintaining and increasing of tenderness of heart. Thus, the disciples did not believe that it was Christ that walked on the sea because they had forgot the "miracles of the loaves, and their hearts were hardened," (Mark 6:52). This seems to be an accidental hardness, discovered in the act.

3. Habitually men's hearts are hardened in sin, when by many acts men are so accustomed to do evil that they

---

[36] *Cor hominis non renativocaturlapideum, Ezek. 11:36; non ferreum, quia 1. Etiamsi serrum durum sit, ut minibus stecti non possir, versariq; sicut cera; habet tamen quandum qualitatem, licet exiguam, ad mollitiem nempe, ut si igni admovenatur, molle fieri queat, et malleum omnem formam stecti, quanquam remaneat ferrum. At lapis nullam habet molitiem, neq; ad mollitiem aptitudinem, ut scilicet adjutus igne mollescere malleoq; stecti posit, permanens lapis; Sio cor nostrum nulla ratione ductile aut flexibile est, ad recti obedien iam, ideoq; opus est, ut totum cor auseratur, et aliud in ejus locum reponatur. 2. Ex lapide nullum unquam liquor exprimi poterit, unde miraculum illud fiat maximum, cum e petia in deserto fluxerunt aquae; sic e corde nostro nihil penitus exprimi potest boni nisi aliud fiat, i.e. elapideo carneum. 3. Lapis non vivit ut caro, nec incorde est aliquid vitae spiritualis, 4. Non ait Deus se transformaturum cor lapid cum in cor carneum; sed ablaturum lapideum et daturum carneum. Significans in natura nostra nihil esse quod astinitatem habeat cum natura Dei, sed opus est ut tota vetus natura tollatur, et nova reponatur.* Zanchius, *de Liber. Arbit. Thess. 9.*

cannot lay it aside; no more than the, "black Moor his skin, or the leopard his spots," (Jer. 13:23). This habitual hardness creeps and steals upon men's spirits through sin's subtlety, which leaves behind it not only *reatum*, guilt, but also *maculum*, a stain or spot—"lest any of you be hardened through the deceitfulness of sin," (Heb. 3:13). This hardness grows on by steps and degrees as divines observe, that is: (1) Their suggestion of sin, (2) Acceptation of the suggestion, (3) Acting in the sin accepted, (4) Delighting in sin acted, (5) Habit and custom in sin delighted in, (6) Necessity in sin accustomed, and finally, (7) Death, the result of all. "Every man is tempted when he is drawn away of his own lust and enticed. Then when lust hath conceived it bringeth forth sin, and sin when it is finished, bringeth forth death," (Jam. 1:14-15). In this observe these degrees: (1) Lust within, which is the nursery of sin and a tinder to catch at all temptations, (2) Drawing away by it, that is, from God, (3) Enticing, that is, to evil, (4) Lust's corruption, that is, a delightful accepting of the enticement and consent of the will and heart thereto, (5) Bringing forth of sin, that is, into act and execution, (6) Finishing of sin acted, i.e., going on in a course and custom of sinning, it being a further step as Calvin notes, and (7) Death, the due wages of all—the degrees of hardening in sin are so reckoned up by Bernard (if he was the author of that book *de Conscientia*), that is: (i) He that has been accustomed to well-doing is so intolerable to sin, as if in sinning he were going down to hell alive, (ii) Of unsupportable in a short time it becomes heavy, (iii) Of heavy, light, (iv) Of lightsome, delightsome, (v) Of delightsome, desirable, (vi) Of desirable customary, (vii) Of customary, excusable, (viii) Of excusable, defensible, and (ix) Of defensible, a matter of boasting. To this height nothing can be added. Nothing so much exasperates the majesty of that dreadful judge as to sin, and securely to sin, and to boast of vices as though they were virtues.[37]

4. Judicially men's hearts are hardened in sin, when they are forsaken of God and given up to their own obduration and the dominion of the devil, that seeing they will be hard they shall be hard with a witness. So, we read often of God's hardening of Pharaoh's heart, (Exod. 4:22, 7:3), and that God, "hardeneth whom he will," (Rom. 9:18). Pharaoh had many judgments upon him, but his hard heart was the most dreadful of all his judgments. This was the plague of his plagues; this is the plague of his soul; a plague that would stick upon him to all eternity.

But when God is said in his judgments to harden men's hearts, we must understand it wisely, cautiously, God hardens no man's heart by infusing any new wickedness in it as the heretics the Manichees wickedly imagined, (Jam. 1:13). For

---

[37] *Perfectum inaq; peccatum non intelligo unum aliquod opus perpetratum, sed cursum peccandi completum.* Calvin *in loc.* Bernard l, *de Conscientis.*

then God should be the author of sin (which is blasphemous to think but once). But God hardens the heart: (1) By withdrawing or denying to the heart his softening grace (which he is *not* bound to give). By this, the heart might be restrained from sin, which grace being denied, the sinner hardens his own heart by his own inward depravity; as when an owner denies to prop up or repair a ruinous, reeling house, the house falls by its own ponderousness. So, divines make God, *causum removentem prohibens*, a cause removing the impediment, of such sins, as men rush upon when their hold-back is removed; (2) By delivering men up to the swing of their own lust, and the dominion of Satan. Compare these places: Psalm 81:11-12; Rom. 1:26-28; 1 Kings 22:22-23, and John 13:26-27. In such case God says that he who is filthy let him be filthy still, and he that is hard-hearted let him be hard-hearted; (3) By giving man means of restraint, which falling upon hearts so forsaken of God, exasperate and enlarge them all the more in all wickedness with violence and greediness; as the stopping or damming up of a violent torrent, makes its streams more impetuous. Not that these restraints provoke to sin properly and formally in their own nature; but occasionally and accidentally only through hard-hearted men's abuse. So, the law irritates sin, "works in them all manner of concupiscence," (Rom. 7:8). Thus, the prophets and ministers of the word harden some men accidentally, (Isa. 6:9-

10 with Acts 28:26-27), which soften others; as the same sun which softens wax, hardens clay; the same heavenly heat which makes a garden of flowers smell more fragrantly, makes sinks or dunghills scents more loathsome; and (4) By denying to hard-hearted men even those means of restraint after those means have been thus miserably abused; but wholly leaving them to the calamity of their own ways, (see Hos. 4:14).[38] So much in brief of the nature of hardness of heart.

Now in the next place, consider how odious a hard heart is to God, and consequently, how odious and burdensome it should be to all God's people. The hatefulness and odiousness of a hard heart to God appears plainly in diverse respects, that is, in that he: (1) Forbids it, (2) Grieves at it, (3) Brands it, (4) Threatens it, and (5) plagues it. Take a taste of all these out of the word.

---

[38] *Non indurate dues imperticudo malitiam; sed non impertiendo misercordiam, Augustine Epistle 105. Sed quomodo punit dues indurarione? Non solum sustentat durum Cor hominis; praescit ejus duritiem; homini contumaciter forenter se opponenti subtrahit suam gratiam; permittit eum ferri suis cupiditatibus; Sed etiam Santanae talem hominem tradit, a quo efficacitur induretur; ut homini in potestatem diaboli tradioto offert verbum, idq; subinde inculcat, nec tamen aliud quicquam esticit, quam ut peccator fiat deterior; Differt insuper paenas, qui dei ad majorem indurationem homo pessime abutitur; Tandem etiam justitiam suaro, in poena induratorum oftendit. Sic ergo inurat dues, non ut peccato author, ne cut otiosus spectator, sed ut justissimus judex. Gerb. Loc. Com. Tom. I de Providentia paragraph 119.*

1. God forbids it in his word; *cry and harden not your hearts*, (see Psalm 95:8, Heb. 3:8-15, 4:7). What God forbids is displeasing and hateful to him.

2. God lays much to the heart, the hardness of men's hearts. Jesus Christ looked round about upon the Pharisees with anger, "being grieved for the hardness of their hearts," (Mark 3:5). And after his resurrection he upbraided his own disciples for the hardness of their hearts, in that they did not believe them that had seen Christ after he was risen, (Mark 16:14)—yes—God professes he was grieved with hard-hearted Israel for 40 years together, (Heb. 3:8-10).

3. God brands hardness of heart with such notes of infamy and disgrace, as discover his great detestation of it. Among many other passages, hardness of heart is accounted of God a fruit and proper effect of sin; "Lest your hearts be hardened through the deceitfulness of sin," (Heb. 3:13), such as is the cause, such is the proper effect, both abominable to God.

Hardness of heart is accounted a great sin itself, whereby God is much "tempted and provoked," (Heb. 3:8-10). The depth of a man's natural misery under sin is laid down under the notion of having a "stony heart," (Ezek. 11:19-20, 36:26-27). The height of Pharaoh's sin is comprised under his "hardness of heart," (Exod. 14:4).

Yes, hardness of heart is a cause of sin of any of the foulest abominations; what temptation of the devil will a hard heart not swallow down, what horrid impieties will a hard heart not rush furiously upon? (See that passage in 2 Kings 17:14). This is as a wicked devil that brings along many other devils with it, to possess the soul. More especially, it brings forth the cursed fruits of: (1) Woeful impenitency, a hard heart cannot, will not, repent, (2 Chron. 36:13; Rom. 2:5); (2) Willful rebellion, pride, and obstinacy against God, (Dan. 5:2; Neh. 9:16-29; Jer. 7:26; Ezek. 3:7); and (3) Willful and damnable unbelief (Acts 19:9; Mark 6:51-52, 8:16-17, 16:14; Heb. 3:8-11, 18:19).[39]

4. God threatens hardness of heart with sad and heavy commination (as Prov. 28:14 and notably Prov. 29:10, Jer. 19:15, but most remarkably, Heb. 3:8-12). God's threats argue evidently God's wrath against it.

5. Finally, over and beyond all this, God plagues hardness of heart with dreadful judgments, whoever hardened himself against God and prospered? (Job 9:4). (1) What temporal vengeance does he inflict for hardness of heart? As

---

[39] *Quid est cor durum? Ipsum est quod nec compunctione scinditur, nec pietate mollitur, nec movetur precibus, minis non cedit, flagellis duratur, ingratum est ad beneficia, infidum ad consilia, saevum ad judicia; inverecundum ad turpia impavidum adpericula, inhumanum ad humana, temerarium ad divina, praeteritorum obliviscens, praeserrium negligens, secura non provideus; ipsum est, cui praeteritorum praeter solas injurias nihil ommino non praeterit; futurorum nulla, nisi forte ad ulciscendum, prospectio est.* Bernard.

upon pharaoh and the Egyptians, who after all their plagues for hardening their hearts against God, were at once entombed in the Red Sea, (Exod. 14), upon Israel, for their hardness of heart, not suffered to enter into God's rest, to enjoy the promised Canaan, (Heb. 3:8-11), and afterwards, they that came into the promised land, for this wickedness were removed out of God's sight, (2 Kings 17:14-18). How terrible was that vengeance of God upon Nebuchadnezzar hardened in his pride? (Dan. 5:20-21); read it and tremble at it. (2) What spiritual wrath does God pour out upon hard hearts? Giving them up to utter obduration, as in Pharaoh, (Exod. 4:22, 7:3, and in others, John 12:40). (3) Finally, what eternal vengeance do hard hearts here treasure up to themselves against the day of wrath? (Rom. 2:5). Doubtless, if God in this way forbids, so to lay to heart and brand, and threaten, and plague a hard heart. A hard heart, though it is never so pleasing to man, or grateful to Satan, yet it is most hateful and abominable to the great heart-searching God. How woeful their condition that lie under the plague of a hard heart! How happy are they that are delivered from it!

    This may serve to put us all upon the trial and examination of our hearts and spirits whether they are broken or not; so that we may discover whether they are the grateful sacrifices of God or not? Which of us would not be glad that our hearts and spirits might be truly acceptable to God? Then let us diligently inquire whether they are truly broken and contrite. The stress of our comfort will peculiarly lean upon this basis of penitential brokenness; if our hearts are actually broken this day, what an odor of a sweet smell shall they be to God continually? But all will depend upon this, that they are kindly broken and softened as David's was.

But how may we discover whether our hearts and spirits are truly broken and contrite? Answer: Principally two ways: (1) By the concomitants or companions of a broken spirit, and (2) By the adjuncts or properties of it.

1. By the concomitants or companions attending upon a broken spirit, *noscitur ex comite, qui non dignoscitur ex se*, oftentimes a man is known by his companions, more than by his own conditions. All the graces of the spirit are spiritually concatenated and linked together; but some graces being more peculiarly homogeneal and near of kin to one another, are more immediately coupled and associated, and such do mutually descry and discover one another.

Now these are the usual and familiar companions of true brokenness of spirit and tenderness of heart, *that is,*

1. A spirit of prayer and supplication—a broken spirit is a praying spirit; they usually go together; they are promised together, "I will pour the spirit of grace and supplication, and they shall look upon me whom they have pierced, and they shall mourn for him," (Zech. 12:10-14). They are performed

together; when the heart of the prodigal son was touched and broken for his lewd courses, presently he resolves upon praying, "I will go to my father and say to him, Father I have sinned against heaven and before thee," (Luke 15:18). Saul (who afterward was called Paul) was no sooner dismounted, struck to the earth, and his heart humbled and broken at his first conversion by Christ's immediate voice from heaven, but Christ gives this character of him, "Behold he prayeth," (Acts 9:11), this was worth beholding and considering indeed, that a persecuting Saul should so soon become a praying saint. Yes, Jesus Christ himself being so broken and abased in his spirit with surrounding sorrow in his agony, [ἐκτενέστερον], "he prayed more fervently," (Luke 22:44). He did as it were bend all his nerves, intend the utmost activity of his spirit, to wrestle with his heavenly father. The apostle says, "he offered up prayers and supplications with strong crying and tears," (Heb. 5:7). Some writings cannot be read but in water, and those petitions of believers which are indicted by the spirit with sobs and groans and swimming along towards God in streams of tears, how legible and available are they with God? "The spirit itself helpeth our infirmities," (Rom. 8:26). No spirit can sigh and groan, can weep and mourn, can tug and wrestle with God like a broken spirit. Such a spirit, not so much prays to God, as powers out itself, and all its desires into the bosom of God, (see Psalm 102). Such a spirit prays importunately, pathetically, powerfully; of all frames of souls, this melting broken frame of spirit is most ingenuous, eloquent, and potent in prayer, fetches arguments from the best topics, God's nature, Christ's merit, covenant, promises, *etc.*, fills itself full of them as a vessel with new wine; urges, darts them up vigorously, pursues the Lord, will let him have no rest, will have no say resolves like Jacob not to let him go until he reach out a blessing. Reflect now upon yourself, O Christian, where is your spirit of supplication? Where are those mighty unutterable groans and desires? Where those wrestlings, *etc.*, do you now know what a spirit of prayer means? Neither do you know what a broken spirit means.[40]

2. Humility—a broken spirit is a humble spirit, low in its own eyes, thinks worse of itself than of any others, or than any others can think of it; can prefer the meanest saint before itself, counting itself the lease of saints, if a saint at all, *etc.* "But to this man will I look, even to him that is poor, and of a contrite spirit," (Isa. 66:2); Poverty of spirit and brokenness of a spirit are familiar companions. Again God says, "I dwell in the high and holy place with him also that is of a contrite and humble spirit," (Isa. 57:15). Here humility and contrition is very inconsistent with a broken spirit, the angel of the church that proudly bragged that he was rich and increased with

---

[40] *Oratio justi clavis est caeli ascendit proecatio, et descendit dei miseratio. Fletus cuius audit quam voces.* Augustine *Sermon 226 de Temp.*

goods and had need of nothing; was afar from brokenness of heart, as he was from apprehensiveness of his own misery, not knowing that he was, "wretched and miserable and poor and blind and naked," (Rev. 3:17). Where now is your humility and spiritual poverty? If you are hardened in spiritual pride, self-conceit, *etc.*, how should a broken spirit lodge in your breast?

3. Love to Jesus Christ—a broken spirit is a tender affectionate loving spirit, and the love of such a spirit flames out most ardently towards Christ. O! the entirety of Christ's love for such a spirit; he prayed for it, bled for it, died for it, and "washed it from its sin in his own blood," (Gal. 2:20, Rev. 1:5). How it esteems, effects, and embraces the Lord! Christ says that you are his portion in the land of the living: Whom have I in heaven but you? And in earth there is none that I can desire besides you? All things are but loss and dung to the winning of Christ, (Phil. 3). One Christ is worth ten thousand words, *etc.* See how strong the love of that penitent broken-hearted woman was to Christ, her bathing his feet in her tears, wiping them with her hair, kissing them with her mouth, and anointing them with costly ointment, palpably proclaiming her love to Christ, and Christ himself testifies that "she loved much," (Luke 7:37-38, 44-49). She could not choose, for Christ loved her much; he forgave her sins which were many, and she gave him her affections and tears which were many. No wonder that a broken heart is a Christ-loving heart; for, it's

Christ that loves, comforts, and binds up the broken heart, (Isa. 61:1-2; Luke 4:18-19). There's much of Christ in the broken heart. How then can a broken heart choose but to be endeared to Christ? As the soaking April showers make the fields send forth a sweet smell, or as the bruising of chamomile makes it the more fragrantly odoriferous; so Christ softening and bruising the heart, makes the heart express a sweet fragrancy of love to him. See now what tender affection you bear to Jesus Christ, to his person, presence, office, honor, and ordinances; image in his members, *etc.*, if you would read brokenness in your heart.

    4. Obedience—a broken spirit is a dutiful, tractable, and obedient spirit. So these two are coupled together: *And I will give them a heart of flesh*—there is the brokenness of spirit—*that they may walk in my statutes and keep my ordinances and do them*—there is obedience associated to brokenness of heart, (Ezek. 11:19-20, 36:26-27); softened wax will receive any impression, melted metal will run into any mold. So a melted, softened heart will bend and bow as God will have it. Then a persecuting Saul can say, "Lord, what wilt thou have me to do? (Acts 9:6). As if he should say, Lord do what you command, I am ready to obey. Then the betrayers and murderers of Christ can say, "Men and brethren what shall we do?" (Acts 2:37). As if they had said, we see that we are

undone in ourselves by our sins, but now we are ready to take any course for remedy, which the Lord by you shall prescribe. Such a heart is fixed and resolved upon all dutiful compliance with God's commands and can say as St. Augustine, "Lord, give me ability to do what you command and then command me whatever you please." Have you such a flexible, dutiful spirit? A broken spirit is an obedient spirit. But a hard heart, like a stone, will not bow or bend, may sooner be ground to powder. Hardened Pharaoh professed, "he would not let Israel go," (Exod. 5:2). Hard-hearted Manasseh and the people would not hearken to God's messages, (2 Chron. 33:10). The stubborn and stony spirited Jews tell Jeremiah plainly, "As for the word that thou hast spoken to us in the name of the Lord, we will not hearken unto thee: but we will certainly do whatsoever thing goeth forth out of our own mouth," (Jer. 44:16-17).[41]

    2. By the adjuncts or properties of a truly penitential, broken spirit, we may further discover whether our spirits are broken, and thereupon, the grateful sacrifices of God. Among the many properties that might be insisted upon, take a taste of these few that follow.

    1. A broken spirit grieves and mourns for the sins of others, especially for the public abounding sins of the times in

---

[41] *Da quod jubes, et jube quod vis.* Augustine's *Confessions* I.l.I.c.13.

which it lives. A soft heart is like the moist elements of water and air, which are very hardly kept in and contained within their own bounds; it satisfies not only itself within the bounds of its own sins to lament them, but runs abroad also in lamentations for others. This, as Augustine expresses it, is *pia tristitia et beata miseria, i.e.*, a pious sorrow and blessed misery to be afflicted for, not to be entangled with other's vices, *etc*. In this way that Phoenix, King Josiah's heart, was tender, and he mourned and wept and rent his clothes for the sins of the land, (2 Chron. 34). King David was a man after God's own heart, and his heart was habitually tender and broken, and how was he affected and afflicted at the sins of others; he says, "I beheld the transgressors and was grieved; because they kept not thy Word," (Psalm 119:158). And again, "Horror hath taken hold upon me: because of the wicked that forsake thy law," (Psalm 1119:53). And yet further, "Rivers of waters run down mine eyes, because they keep not thy Law," (Psalm 119:136). Mark that Josiah's heart was tender; he humbled himself before God; he rent his clothes and wept before the Lord. David expresses his grief, horror, and rivers of tears, and both for other's sins. Here, right honorable, you may see in these two gracious kings that it is a beam of true honor and nobility becoming peers or princes, to have broken spirits that can relent for other's offences. And this is the periphrasis of those tender-hearted saints in Jerusalem. "Men that sigh, and that cry for all the abominations that are done in the midst thereof," (Ezek. 9:4). Whereas a hard heart does not trouble itself at other's sins, but rather, "doth the same, and takes pleasure in them that do them," (Rom. 1:32). How is your heart affected at other's sins, especially at the horrid impieties of these times, where is your grief, your horror, your sight, your cries, your rivers of tears in secret?[42]

2. A broken spirit has clear and sad apprehensions of its own sinfulness; if other's sins are motes, its own are beams; if others are molehills its own are apprehended as mountains. The sins of others are bitter, but its own sins are very wormwood and the gall of bitterness. The eyes of such, like the cherubim's faces, (2 Chron. 3:13), are inward and most intent upon themselves. They "know that in themselves, that is in their flesh dwells no good," (Rom. 7:18), but by nature a mere rendezvous, sin, Sodom, and hell of all sin; original sin being feminally, potentially, and dispositively, all sins; consequently, all imaginations, thoughts, words, and works in that state only evil continually, (Gen. 6:5), and if brought into a state of grace still, "seeing another law in their members warring," (Rom. 7:23), "body of death," (Rom. 7:24), [τοῦ σώματος τοῦ θανάτου τούτου], that "easily encompassing sin,"

---

[42] Pia est ista tristieia, et si dici potest, beata miseria, vitiis alienis tribulari non implicari: dolore contrahi, amore non attrahi, etc. Augustine Epistle 545.

(Heb. 12:1), where not only innumerable swarms of errors, infirmities, *etc.*, and that in the best and most spiritual duties surround them, but too often gross lapses overturn them. These things sadly pondered, deeply wound and perplex broken spirits; so that they are, "pricked in their hearts," (Acts 2:36); they, "mourn and are in bitterness," (Zech. 12:10-11). Their very, "bones are as it were broken," (Psalm 51), and they dolefully groan out with the apostle, "O! wretched men that we are, who shall deliver us from the body of this death," (Rom. 7:24). For these things that sigh, sob, tear, and sorrow pour out before the Lord. Softness of heart making them most sensible of their own corruptions, which while their hearts were hardened they little regarded; as blots run abroad and seem biggest in wet paper; when the, "cockatrice egg is crushed, it breaketh out into a viper," (Isa. 59:5); the viper formerly hid and undiscovered, then appears. So, when the carnal heart is crushed and bruised, then the toads, snakes, vipers, and vermin of sin are evidenced, which until then were not imagined to be there. Philosophers have a maxim: *Grave non gravitat proprio loco,* a heavy thing is not felt heavy in its own place, as water in the sea; but a little of that water out of its proper place is more heavy than can be borne; while the heart is in its hard, sinful state, it's in its element, in its own natural place, sin is no burden; but when the heart becomes spiritually broken for sin and is taken out of its natural condition, then the unsupportable load of sin is felt with a witness. Consider—is all sin bitter; your own sin most bitter—do you cast the first stone at yourself?[43]

3. A broken spirit is most perplexed at sin, as it is against God, as it is against Jesus Christ. To sin against so good a God, so sweet a Savior, oh how this kills a broken spirit! This stabbed David to the heart above all other considerations, that he had sinned against God, "Against thee, thee only have I sinned," (Psalm 51:4). Against you that has made me, maintained me, loved me, delivered me, crowned me, redeemed me, *etc.*; O! against you, you only—what? Had not David sinned against Uriah's life by murdering him? Against Bathsheba's chastity by uncleanness? Against his own body, the temple of the Holy Spirit, by defiling it? (1 Cor. 6:18-19). And against the honor of religion, scandalizing God's people and, "giving great occasion to the enemies of God to blaspheme?" (2 Sam. 12:14). All this is true, nor intended David to deny it, but to show where the point of his grief principally lay; it went most of all to his heart that he had sinned against

---

[43] *Poenitentiam cenam non facit, nisi odium peccati, et amor Dei. Quando sic poenites, ut tibi anuarum sapiat in animo, quod ante dulce fuit in vita; et quod te prius oblectabat in corpore, ipsum te cruciat in mente, jam tunc bene ingermiteis, et dicis ad Deum, Tibi soli pecavi. Augustine sermon 3 de Nat. Dom. Saepe quod torpentes latuit, flentibus innotescit; et astlictamens certius invenit in alum quod fecerat, et retum suum cujus lecura non meminit, hunc in se coromota deprehendit. Greg. lib. S. Mopal.*

such a God. And when the Jews shall be re-implanted into their own flock, this shall most deeply pierce them that they did so cruelly and causelessly pierce Christ. This shall bring them to mourn as for an only son to be in bitterness as for a firstborn to a great mourning as in Hadadrimmon for Josiah that best of kings; to a particular private and serious mourning, "every family apart and their wives apart," (Zech. 12:10-12). Hard hearts are chiefly troubled at fear, shame, or punishment for sin; but nothing more melts a broken spirit than that it has sinned against such matchless love, spurned against melting bowels and offended against such precious blood of such a Savior; O! how it's pricked with Christ's crown of thorns, how it bleeds over Christ's bleeding wounds, and for its tearing open Christ's side and heart, how it could tear itself in pieces!

4. A broken spirit trembles at God's word and at God's rod; when God speaks and when God strikes.

At God's word the broken spirit trembles. "But to this man will I look, even to him that is poor and of a contrite spirit, and trembleth at my word," (Isa. 66:2). He trembles at the promises, lest he should distrust them; at the threats, least he should despise them and involve himself in them; at the commands, lest he should disobey and violate them, *etc.*; O! there is enough in the word of divine Majesty's power and authority to make a giant's heart to quake. Felix the governor trembled before Paul preaching of judgment, *etc.*, and Paul, at that time but a poor prisoner in chains, (Acts 24-25). Did Felix tremble slavishly? How much more do the contrite spirits tremble filially? They that despise, scorn, oppose, and blaspheme the word of God, how far are they from true penitential contrition? (*Nihil formidabilius est, quam non formidare dei minas.* Basil *de Spiritus Sancti.*)

At God's rod also the contrite spirit quakes. How did the repenting people of God in Ezra's days, "tremble because of the great rain?" (Ezra 10:9), and this is the judgment of God that has of late been most extraordinarily inflicted upon this land, for which we are here trembling before the Lord this day. Surely we have great cause to tremble, not only at the plague of waters itself and the sad consequences of scarcity and dearth which may follow, but much more at the wrath of God that appears in it, and the sins of England the procuring cause of it. Yes, a tender heart trembles at the very shaking of God's rod, how did good Josiah's heart melt when God's displeasure against his people did but hang in the threats? (2 Chron. 34:27).

5. Finally, a broken spirit, humbled and wounded truly for sin, sets speedily and seriously upon a real reformation. Upon reformation both private and public, as his place requires and as opportunity is afforded.

A Broken Spirit

Privately, a broken spirit is studious to reform itself, to embrace a new course of life, which as Luther observes, is the best repentance. The prodigal humbled, reforms, goes to his father, bewails, and forsakes his former lewdness, (Luke 15). Saul, humbled by the mighty hand of Christ at his conversion, presently reforms, gives over persecuting of the saints, and, "straightway preaches Christ in the synagogues, that he is the Son of God," (Acts 9:20). After Peter's heart was broken, and he had wept bitterly for his shameful denial of his master, (Matt. 26:75, Luke 22:62); he so reformed himself in this particular that we never after read that he relapsed into the same sin—yes—we read our Savior's prophecy of him that he should glorify God by being himself crucified for Christ and his truth, (John 21:18). (*Optima poenitenua nova vita.* Lueb.)

Publicly, a broken spirit is desirous also to reform others. It is very remarkable in Scriptures that when magistrates and rulers became men of contrite and broken spirits indeed, they could not rest and terminate in personal, but did proceed to public reformation in the kingdom and church wherein they lived. So Ezra hearing of the sins of the people of the land and of the princes by unlawful marriages with the heathens, "rent his garment and mantle, and plucked off the hair of his head and of his beard, and sat down astonied," (Ezra 9:1-3) (here are notable symptoms how his spirit was broken for their sins); consequently, both Ezra and the people were weeping very sore, set upon reformation, to put away all the strange wives and their children, and Ezra made them covenant and swear to God to do it, and after took course to have it done, (Ezra 10:1-5). In this way, good King Josiah's heart being tender, and his spirit melted at consideration of the people's sins, he sets presently and vigorously upon public reformation, makes the law of God to be read publicly, enters into covenant with God to keep his commandments and his testimonies and his statutes with all his heart, and with all his soul—caused all that were present in Jerusalem and Benjamin to stand to it—took away all the abominations out of all the country that pertained to the children of Israel, and made all that were present in Israel to serve, to serve the Lord their God; and all his days they did not depart from following the Lord, the God of their fathers; here was reformation to purpose, (2 Chron. 34:19, 27, 29-33). Yes, Manasseh himself (that prodigious monster of wickedness, 2 Chron. 33:2-11), when in his affliction his heart was broken so that he sought the Lord his God and humbled himself greatly before the God of his fathers. Even then this Manasseh set upon public reformation; for, "he took away all strange gods and idols out of the house of the Lord, and all the altars that he had built in the mount of the house of the Lord and in Jerusalem and cast them out of the city. And, he repaired the altar of the Lord and sacrificed thereon peace-offerings and thank-offerings; and commanded Judah to serve the Lord God of Israel," (2 Chron. 32:12, 15-16). So, he: (1) Removed the abominations, which himself had erected, (2) Restored the pure worship of God, which himself destroyed, and (3) Commanded Judah to serve the Lord God of Israel; who could have expected such a reformation from Manasseh? His humbled spirit could not choose but to reform. Then what church and state need to despair of reformation, if the Lord would but thoroughly humble and break the hearts of princes and rulers, as he did Manasseh?

Right honorable, this in special concerns you, be pleased to consider these three famous magistrates, how when their spirits were broken they speedily and seriously testified the same in public reformations; if you get broken hearts like them, you will reform like them. It's true, you and the people have sworn and covenanted with God a public reformation according to the word of God. And God has honored you to lay some foundations of reformation, for which we bless God; hoping that these beginnings will still be carried forward to perfection; and that God will not "despise the day of small things," (Zech. 4:10). But yet both church and state still cry out for further reformation—how does the common-wealth groan under woeful oppression, injustice, and all manner of violence and wrong, as much, if not more than ever? O! hasten to save the poor kingdom from these destructive evils! But how does the church of God, not only groan, but even languish, faint, and die continually under those cursed diseases of error, heresy, blasphemy, licentiousness, divisions, disorder, and confusion, horrid atheism and all manner of profaneness? Are there not among us that say, we have no church, no ministry, no ordinances; that oppose and deny the Scriptures, the immortality of the soul, the divinity of Christ, the deity of the Holy Spirit, and almost all the fundamentals of religion—yes—and all visible outward reformation? Where are we falling? Should these things still pass on without control, what religion shall we leave to our posterity? Can we redress these distempers? Ministers may preach, people may petition, and both may pray; but if you sit still, who are "heirs of restraint," (Judge. 18:7), who bear the sword and should not "bear the sword in vain," (Rom. 13), where shall we have healing? You have power to hinder, you have sworn to extirpate these evils, if they are not extirpated; we may justly fear they will extirpate both you and us at last. Let it not be said of these lewd persons, as once of Eli's sons: *They have made themselves vile, but you restrained them not*; you know it's an old maxim in divinity, *Qui cum possit, non prohibet, jubet*. "He that can, but does not hinder evil, commands it." God forbid you should contract such guilt upon yourselves; besides these evils to be removed, are they not many necessary parts of reformation lacking? As the public confession of faith and catechism, besides many things in church government? O! that the perfecting of these might be accelerated! O! gird on zeal, be valiant for the truth, accomplish the reformation, imitate those broken-hearted reformers; never let it be said that you should come short of King Manasseh. Be strong and the Lord shall be with you.

This doctrine may serve to exhort all persons that desire either this day or at any time hereafter to present the Lord with sacrifices acceptable indeed, that they get and keep broken spirits. These are the sacrifices of God; these he will not despise, but without these all your professions, prayers, duties, *etc.*, will be utterly rejected.

But how shall we get and keep broken spirits? *Hic labor, hoc opus est.* Here is the difficulty.

Answer: A broken spirit may be obtained and maintained.

1. By a due dependence upon God alone in Jesus Christ for a broken spirit, without God and Christ, you cannot break your own heart, nor can all the world do it for you, you may as well think to hold the winds in your fist from blowing and the waves of the sea from rolling up and down and roaring; to span the vast ocean with your fingers; to hold the huge globe of the earth in the hollow of your hand and to stop the course

of the sun and moon in the firmament; as to instill into your own heart true penitential brokenness. Only, "God gives repentance," (2 Tim. 2:25). Only God that made the heart can melt and mend the heart. It's his sole prerogative both, "to take away the heart of stone and to give a heart of flesh," (Ezek. 11:19, 36:26). (1) God can enlighten and convince the heart of its own hardness; (2) God can subdue and remove the heart's stoniness; (3) God can infuse a habitual supernatural tenderness; and (4) God can draw forth this habit into actual relentings upon all good occasions; this is his method. God alone can do all in this matter, rely only on him for it, as its sole author.

2. By a dutiful attendance upon God's word in its powerful ministry; this is most, "quick and powerful and sharper than any two-edged sword, piercing even to the dividing asunder of soul and spirit," (Heb. 4:12). Are our hearts iron? The word is as fire to soften and melt the iron. Are our hearts stone? The word is, "as a hammer to break the rock in pieces," (Jer. 23:29). This instrumentally made King Josiah's heart tender, (2 Chron. 34:19-27). This made the returned exiles to weep, (Neh. 8:9). This pricked Peter's hearers in their hearts, (Acts 2:26). O! wait upon this word of God with a lively heart-searching ministry. O! tremble at this mighty working word of God that can through God make a hard heart soft and keep a soft heart tender.

3. By a frequent and serious consideration of our own and others' sins. Others' sins may break our hears, as it is clear in the case of Josiah, (2 Chron. 34:19; of David, Psalm 119:59, 158, 136; of Ezra, Ezra 9:1-5; and of those mourners, Ezek. 9:4). But our own sins may even grind our hearts to powder, as appears here in David, "My sin is ever before me—against thee, thee only have I sinned—that the bones which thou hast broken," (Psalm 51:3-4, 8); as in the prodigal, (Luke 15:18-19), and as in those Jews, (Zech. 12:10-12), man's sin makes the whole creation groan, as under a load ready to break its back, (Rom. 8:22), and shall not man's own spirit groan and his own heart break under the pressure of his own iniquities? In what words shall I, a little, represent the sins of England and the sins of your own souls to you for the actual mollifying of your hearts?

Think what sin is; it is the transgression of the law, (1 John 3:4); the death of the soul, (Eph. 2:1); the fruits of the flesh, (Gal. 5:19); the works of the devil, (1 John 2:8); and utter abomination to God, (Prov. 26:25). Sin is so foul and filthy that the filth under the nails and armholes, (Jam. 1:21); the vomit of a dog, the mire of a swine, (2 Peter 2:22); the poison of serpents, (Rom. 3:13); the spots of leopards and the skin of black Moors, (Jer. 13:23); the putrification and deadly stink of opened sepulchers, (Rom. 3:13); and basest excrements themselves, (Jam. 1:21); are the similitude wherein the Holy

Spirit sets it out to us. Sin is the inlet of death and all misery, (Rom. 5:12), worse than the devil, for sin made him a devil; and the very hell of hell.

Think against whom sin is committed. Against God blessed forever, infinitely pure and cannot look upon it, (Heb. 1:13). He is just and will not clear the guilty, (Exod. 34:7), omniscient, knows all sin fully, and omnipotent, can crush all sinners eternally. He fashioned you curiously; he has provided for you plentifully, has given Christ his own Son to redeem and save you to the uttermost, has loved you freely, and has always been doing you good; he never did you harm and against him you have often wondered—O! how this wounded David, (Psalm 51). Against Christ also you sin, who became man—yes—a man of sorrows—yes—a worm rather than a man for you. Who was tempted, betrayed, scorned, abused, bruised, and wounded for you; who prayed, sighed, sorrowed, sweat drops of blood, and poured out his soul to death for you; "who loved thee and washed thee from thy sins in his own blood, (Rev. 1:5). How should this make you mourn, (Zech. 12:10-12). Yes, against the Spirit that convinces, illuminates, adopts, sanctifies, seals, comforts, and dwells in you. Is this your kindness to your God? Do you in this way requite the Lord, O! foolish and unwise person?

Think by whom sin is acted, by them that are to God but as worms, moths, grasshoppers, as the dust of the balance, as nothing, as chaff before the wind, and as stubble before the consuming fire. Your sins do not hurt God, but yourselves. If you are holy, what do you do to him? If sinful, what do you do against him? (Job 35:6).

Think how your sins, England's sins are aggravated, being beyond sins of Sodom, Samaria, and Jerusalem because against greater light, mercies, means, and ordinances than ever they enjoyed against promises and threats, kindness and judgments, and the patience of God, wonderful deliverances, and a glorious Gospel. How should such confide rations as these even break the soul in pieces!

4. By a prudent laying to the heart of God's judgments inflicted. This may be a means of softening a stony heart, when perhaps the word will not penetrate. Manasseh, who would not hearken to God's word, yet melted in his chains and, "humbled himself greatly," (2 Chron. 33:12). How did the people, "tremble at the greater rain?" (Ezra 10:9). God implies that his judgments will make the, "uncircumcised hearts be humbled, and accept the punishment," (Lev. 26:41), and bring people to, "know the plague in their own heart," (1 Kings 8:38). Consider now how God has plagued England with his judgments and let your hearts be broken for England and yourselves in it.

Think what variety of judgments are upon the land. The pestilence has slain thousands, the sword ten thousands.

The immoderate rain for these diverse months hindering seedtime with some, or washing seed sown out of the ground, with others; and so threatening a famine. The murrain among horses and cattle in some places (as is credibly reported) and which is heavier than all, the spirit of error and heresy that spreads and frets among us as a gangrene; so many being given up to strong delusion to believe a lie, (2 Thess. 2:11). How are these judgments linked together and pursue one another as Job's messengers and the billows of the sea? And God's hand is stretched out *still*.

Think of the impartiality of God's judgment upon us. No degree, sex, or age has been spared. King and subject, nobles and ignoble, magistrates and ministers, high and low, and rich and poor all have tasted of God's severity.

Think of God's wrath and displeasure that discovers itself in all, his frown more heavy than that frowns of all the world, if he looks but upon the earth, it trembles, if he touches the hills, they smoke, (Psalm 104:32), and shall we not tremble when he is angry?

Think of England's sins deserving all these and worse; these shafts that fall upon our heads we first shot up against heaven ourselves—no—it's the Lord's mercies that England is not consumed as Jerusalem said of herself, (Lam. 3:22).

O! how is truth, peace, and union among brothers, health and our many comforts broken? And shall our hard hearts only remain unbroken?

5. Finally, by deliberate contemplations upon God's mercies to England and to us. The love, kindness, and mercies of God to man are accustomed to thaw and melt men's hearts for their unkindness to God, here Ezra labors so to break his own and his people's hearts by the overcoming mercies of God repeated, (Ezra 9: 7-13). That your hearts may be softened with mercies, seriously ponder upon and amplify to yourselves personal mercies, parliamentary mercies, and kingdom mercies.

What comfort does this doctrine afford to all truly broken spirits and contrite hearts! These are God's sacrifices; these God will not despise, and then, who shall despise them?

Such hearts God prefers beyond all legal sacrifices, (Psalm 51:16, 17:2), beyond all pharisaical duties and perfections, (Luke 18:3). In these he has most favorable respect, (Isa. 66:2-4), of such he is the peculiar physician, (Psalm 147:3; Isa. 61: 1-5), with such he himself will dwell, (Isa. 57:15), and where God dwells, there light, life, grace, glory, peace, comfort, happiness, and heaven itself to dwell also. Happy hearts are in this way grateful to God.

FINIS

God's Afflicting Providence and Other Works

INTRODUCTION TO THE CHRISTIAN'S ADVANTAGE BOTH BY LIFE AND DEATH

Discovered in a sermon preached at the funeral of that
Faithful and eminent servant of the Lord,
Joseph Jackson, late esq., and alderman of the city of Bristol,
On the 17th day of January, 1661 A.D.

By Francis Roberts, D.D.
Rector of the church at Wrington in the county of Somerset.

"To me to live is Christ, and to die is gain," (Phil. 1:21)

Hieronym. ad. Eustoch, in Epitaph. Paulae, tom 1.
Non moeremus, quod talem amisimus; Sed gratias agimus, quod habuimus, imo habemus. Deo enim vivunt omnia; et quicquid revertitur ad Dominum, in familiae numero computatur.
Heironym. ad Thedor. in Epitaph, Lucinii, tom. 1.
Nos dolendi magis, qui quotidie stamus in praelio peccatorum, vitiis sordidamur, accipimus vulnera, et de otoso verbo reddituri sumus rationem.

LONDON,
Printed by Edward Mottershed.
1662.

The Christian's Advantage Both by Life and Death

To my much honored and entirely beloved friends in the Lord,

The children, brothers, sisters, and others in near and dear relation to Joseph Jackson, late esq., and alderman of the city of Bristol, now sleeping in Jesus; yes, living and triumphing in bliss with Jesus; grace, mercy, and peace in this life and eternal glory in the life to come.

My dear Christian friends,

How brittle, frail, and failing is the most flourishing life of man here on earth! The holy Scriptures compute it by 70 or 80 years, (Psalm 90:10), by a few years, (Job 16:22), by months, (Job 14:1), by one day, (Job 14:6), by all denoting the extreme brevity of it. And they compare his life and time of abode here below to a vanishing vapor, (Jam. 4:14), to a transient wind, (Job 7:7), to a perishing puff of breath, (Psalm 146:4; Isa. 2:22), to a fading flower, (Psalm 103:15-16; Job 14:2), to a momentary meditation thought or tale told, (Psalm 90:9), to withering grass, (Psalm 90:5-6; 1 Peter 1:24), to a speedy irrevocable flood, (Psalm 90:5), to yesterday when past and gone, (Psalm 90:4), to a hastening post, (Job 9:25), to a swift weaver's shuttle, (Job 7:6), to short handbreadths, (Psalm 39:5), to a weaver's web, soon brought to the thrum to be cut off, (Isa. 38:12), to a watch in the night, but three hours long,

(Psalm 90:4), to a vanishing shadow, (Job 4:2, 8:9; Psalm 102:11), to crumbling dust, (Psalm 103:14), to a sleep insensibly passing, (Psalm 90:5), to an apparition or image, (Psalm 39:6). And (as if all these have not reached home) to mere nothing, (Psalm 39:5). By all these, emphatically describing the extreme lubricity, uncertainty, and vanity of man's life. Whereupon we may with the psalmist justly conclude; surely, every man at his best state is altogether vanity. Selah, (Psalm 39:5). Not only man, but every man; not in some state only, as of childhood, sickness, old age, *etc.*, but at his best state, (Heb.), when settled; is not only vain, but vanity itself; not only vanity in part, or in some regard, but in whole altogether vanity; and all this with a (surely) prefixed for the more undoubted certainty; and with a (Selah) suffixed, for the greater observableness.[44]

It is not long since his late dear yokefellow was by nature's dissolution divorced from him; and now himself is by death separated and removed from you. O! what is man? Little did I think to have preached at the funeral of either; and lo, so has the Lord disposed things, that I have (not without much reluctancy and grief) performed this last office for them both, not many years interposing. They have prevented both you

---

[44] *These resemblances I am wont to express in this ensuing memorial: Vita, vapor, ventus, flatus, flos, fabula, faenum, flumen, heris cursor, radius, palmaria, textum, Excubiae, umbra, cinis, somnus, imago, nihil.*

and me; our work is to prepare to follow after. The good Lord teaches us to number our days that we may apply our hearts to wisdom, (Psalm 90:12). To true spiritual wisdom, to wisdom for ourselves, for our souls, for our eternal estate with our dearest Savior Jesus Christ in heaven. We have here no continuing city; let us diligently seek the one to come; a city that has foundations, whose builder and maker is God, (Heb. 13:14, 11:10). Let us so manage our earthly pilgrimage that we may make sure of the heavenly heritage; let us improve this mortality, as not to miss of that immortality; and so live on earth awhile that we may undoubtedly live in heaven forever. (Mary his late wife deceased April 24 and was buried May 5, 1657. Joseph Jackson himself slept in the Lord Jan. 5 and was interred Jan. 17, 1661.)

As for you that are surviving, my conscience and affection (I cannot but affectionately love those that belong to him, whom I so intensively affected for Christ in him) prompt me to present a few requests to you by way of advice; and I hope you will resent them with Christian acceptation.

1. Be pleased to peruse and practice those ten instructions or practical directions published in my instructive and hortatory epistle prefixed to my sermon preached at the funeral of Mary Jackson, his late religious yokefellow. You have the printed books and directions; I need not mention any particulars, but compendiously refer you to

them. I heartily recommend them to your faithful practice; beseeching the God of all wisdom to give you salvifical understanding in all things.[45]

2. Endeavor to comfort yourselves in this your great loss of him and deep affliction for him, by Christian considerations. And what consolatory arguments may you not readily suggest to yourselves? His life was so Christian, that his death needs to be comfortable. Of a good life there cannot come a bad death; as of a bad life seldom comes a good death. Life and death were his, for all manner of spiritual advantages. He lived to the Lord and died to the Lord; both living and dying, he was and is the Lord's, (Rom. 14:8). His body (as Hierom said of Nepotianus) is returned to the earth; but his soul is restored to Christ. His sins and sorrows are all ended; his graces are perfected and his eternal joys are begun. While you are lamenting in black, he is triumphing in white. Are we born (that I may use Hierom's words to Paula upon the death of her daughter Blesilla) that we should here abide eternally? Abraham, Moses, Isaiah, Peter, James, John, Paul the chosen vessel, and above all, the Son of God die. And are we grieved that one depart the body, whose soul was accepted of God, as to be snatched out of the midst of iniquity and error? Let that dead person be lamented, whom hell receives, whom the

---

[45] The sermon is entitled, *The Checkerwork of God's Providences Towards his own People*, London, 1657, and is contained in the first chapter of this work.

infernal pit devours, for whose punishment everlasting fire burns. As for us whose end the angels accompany, whom Christ meets, let us rather grieve, that we are kept so long in the tabernacle of death, (and may not meet Christ sooner) seeing while we are present in this body, we are absent from the Lord. Let faith, hope, and love be your comforters (as Augustine advised an Italian widow, upon the death of her husband). Faith—for you are not desolate as long as Christ dwells in your hearts by faith. Hope—for you cannot but confidently hope, that he is not lost but only sent before you; that he is in heaven with Christ, which is far best of all, (Phil. 1:23). That at the last day his body shall rise again, to be glorified together with his soul and this forever. And the dead's resurrection is the Christian's confidence and consolation. Love—for the more entirely you loved him while he was with you, the more exceedingly should you rejoice at his happiness, now he is with the Lord. And the time of hastening apace, when all that are Christ's shall meet again and never part anymore.[46]

---

[46] *Qualis vita, finis ita. Corpus terra suscepit; anima Christo reddita est. Hieron. in Epitaph. No potian. p. 29 B. tom. 11. Ad hoc enim nati sumus, ut maneamus aeterni? Abraham, Moses, Esaias, Petrus, Jacobus, Joannes, Paulus electionis vas, et super omnia filius Dei, moritur: Et nos indignamur aliquem exire de corpore, qui ad hoc forsitan raptus est, ne malitia mutaret intellectum ejus? Placita v. Deo erat anima ejus. Propter hoc properavit educere eam de media iniquitate, ne longo vitae itinere, deviis oberraret aufractibus. Lugeatur mortuus, sed ille, luem gehenna suscipit, luem tartarus devorat, in cujus poenam aeternus ignis aestuat. Nos quorum exitum Angelorum turba comitatur,*

3. Turn all your lamentations for him into imitation of him. He was a fair copy to write after; follow him as he followed Christ, (1 Cor. 11:1). I have laid down here after my sermon a short list at his exemplary virtues; both you and I know more of his true Christian worth. Strive to be like him in grace that you may be like him in glory. And you that are sharers in his plentiful earthly estate left behind him, you especially are to be put in remembrance of his great charity, bounty, and liberality, which with that estate he was accustomed to exert upon all good occasions; that you may tread in his steps. The backs and bellies of many and many poor distracted creatures had long and frequent occasions of blessing him. Let them have like causes of blessing you and God for you. So shall they say, "Our almner is not lost, but changed, for the stream of charity is still continued. His alms deeds were doubtless one eminent way of sanctifying all his great enjoyments on earth, (Luke 11:41), and of augmenting his reward in heaven, (1 Tim. 6:17-19; Luke 16:9). And like

---

quibus obviam Christus occurrit; gravemur magis si diutius in tabernaculo isto mortis habitemus; quia quamdiu hic moramur, perigrinamur a Domino. Hieronym. ad Paulam super obitu Blesill e filia, p. 158. D. Tom. 1 Basil 1553. Consoletur autem te Fides, et Spes tua, et insa Charitas—Non enim te desolatam putare debes, cui in interiore homine habeas praesentem Christum per fidem in corde tuo. Aut sic te contristari oportet quemadmodum Gentis quae spem non habent, cum veracissima promissione sper emus nos de hac vita, unde migraturi quosdam nostos migrantes non amisimus, sed [UNKNOWN WORD MARGIN EPISTLE DEDICATORY PAGE 4]—Aug. I placae vid. Epist. 6 ad init tom. 2. Fiducia Christianorum, Resurrectio Mortuorum. Tertullian de Refor. carnis. c.I.

charitable courses in you, shall doubtless be crowned with like happy advantages.[47]

4. Endeavor, I beseech you, with all faithful care, the right Christian and gracious education of his son and daughter, his two small orphans, left in trust among you. You are trustees of the dead, and you are instructed with his choicest jewels, his children; and that not only with their estates and bodies; but especially with their souls. O! study to be faithful to the uttermost, engage them in the true knowledge of God, Jesus Christ, and Christianity; as also in the right religious practice of godliness in various times; that when they are old, they may never depart from it, (1 Chron. 28:9; Eccl. 12:1; Prov. 22:6; Eph. 6:4). God has by his providence made you pro-parents to them; O! still express a Christian parental affection towards them so that at last, in this young Joseph the son, old Joseph the father may in a sort remain alive by inheriting and exerting his father's virtues.[48]

5. Finally, vouchsafe in reference to yourselves to reduce this ensuing sermon into practice. As here both life and death are discovered to be theirs that are Christ's. So in every point endeavor that both may be yours as being Christ's. For particulars I refer you to the sermon itself. It was preached

---

[47] *Egregiae virtutis exempla veluti lumen, in edito ponenda sunt, ut omnibus praeluceant, multosque ad sui emulationem accendant. Erasm. in Episle ad Arch. Tolet. praefix Augustini operitus, p. ult.*

[48] *Quo semel est imbuta recens, servabit odorem, Testadui*—Horat.

under some inevitable confinement to time because the assembly was very great; therefore, here and there I have interposed some few passages for the necessary illustrations of what was then spoken briefly and more obscurely. Love, hope, and fear have at last inclined me to consent to the publication of it. Love, to many Christian friends; whose importunities herein I could not well withstand. Hope, that being made public, it may possibly by directing, comforting, and quickening in some measure, help some poor soul onward in their heavenly journey even after my decease. And fear, except by the help of some imperfect notes taken at the preaching of it, it should have been (as was suggested to me) sent abroad into the world immaturely in an extraneous dress, to my prejudice, and other's disservice. And now, such as it is, I present and dedicate it to you more especially, as a peculiar token of my great respect and love, both to him that is departed and to his that remain. That his blessed memory may yet live a little among you in these my ensuing lines: And that you may yet further be incited so to live and die, as that after death, you may live with Christ and with him and with all that are Christ's eternally,[49] which is the earnest desire and prayer of,

---

[49] *Illum nostra pagella decantet; Illum nostrae literae sonent. Quem corpore non valemus, recordatione teneamus: Et cum quo loqui non postumus, de eo loqui nunquam desinamus. Heronym in Epitaph. Nepat. p.27. infin. tom. I.*

Your affectionate brother, friend, and servant in the Lord; for the furtherance of your faith and joy,

Francis Roberts

Wrington, from my study, Feb. 20, 1661.

THE SERMON:
A True Christian's Manifold Advantage in Christ, Both in Life and Death

"ὥστε μηδεὶς καυχάσθω ἐν ἀνθρώποις· πάντα γὰρ ὑμῶν ἐστιν, 22 εἴτε Παῦλος εἴτε Ἀπολλῶς εἴτε Κηφᾶς, εἴτε κόσμος εἴτε ζωὴ εἴτε θάνατος, εἴτε ἐνεστῶτα εἴτε μέλλοντα· πάντα ὑμῶν, 23 ὑμεῖς δὲ Χριστοῦ, Χριστὸς δὲ θεοῦ," (1 Cor. 3:21-23).

"For all things are yours; Whether Paul...or the world, or life, or death, or things present, or things to come; all are yours; And ye are Christ's; and Christ is God's," (1 Cor. 3:21-23).

Who does the apostle speak of concerning these high things? Of them that are sanctified in Christ Jesus called to be saints. For to such he wrote this excellent epistle, (1 Cor. 1:2). What? Are all things theirs, whether Paul, or Apollos, or Cephas, or the world, or life, or death, or things present, or things to come; are all theirs? And they Christ's? And Christ God's?

Happy are the people that are in such a case! Yes, three times happy is that people whose God in Christ is the Lord, (Psalm 144:15).

Some think and say that they are rich and increased with goods and have need of nothing; who yet do not know that they are wretched, miserable, poor, blind, and naked, (Rev. 3:17). But here they that are Christ's are declared to be rich indeed by Christ; forasmuch as in Christ and through Christ, all things are theirs.

The words are very emphatic, comprehensive, and mysterious. Let us view them in their: (1) Connection, (2) Contents, and (3) propositions then resulting.

1. The connection of these words with the context is hinted in the particle γὰρ, *for*, (1 Cor. 3:21). This particle has various uses in the New Testament. It is: (1) Sometimes expletive, denoting the mere emphasis of any expression or phrase, (as in Matt. 1:18; 2 Tim. 2:7); (2) Sometimes declarative, setting forth some matter or thing more fully, (as in Luke 2:10; 1 Thess. 2:14); and often (3) Causal and argumentative, giving a reason for confirmation of anything propounded or asserted, (as in Rom. 14:7-9). And in this sense it's used here, (1 Cor. 3:21), as a reason *why* the Corinthians should not glory in men, in any of their ministers, because they and the church were not for the ministers, but the ministers and all things for them; and they for Christ, *etc.*, (1 Cor. 3:21). And the argument seems to be *a majori ad minus affirmative*, from the greater to the lesser affirmatively. So, Christ is God's, you are Christ's and all things are yours, for your good, for your happiness. All things (as Beza well

illustrates it) are yours, as your helps and furtherances to Christ and by Christ to God. And consequently, all your teachers with all their variety and eminency of gifts are yours also. Therefore, you must not acquiesce, nor finally rest in any of these; you must not terminate nor glory in any of them; but only in Christ and in God. Otherwise, (as Beza well expresses it), they are not so much yours, but rather you are theirs.[50]

These Corinthians carnally gloried in the gifts of their teachers, some in one respect, some in another; whereupon contentions and divisions increased among them, (1 Cor. 1:10-12). Therefore, Paul, by many arguments and by this in the text after the rest, endeavors to quench these heats and to cure these unchristian distempers.

But I may not any further look back to the context having many steps to make forward in the text. Nor do I intend to handle these words in their relative, but in their more absolute consideration.

2. The contents wrapped up in these words are most observable and eminent. *For,*

In this is a rich magazine of treasure. And this treasure is especially tripartite, *that it is,*

---

[50] Sic John Calvin, *in comment ad 1 Cor. 3:21-23; id est, adminicula vobis destinata, ut ad Christum, et a Christo ad Deum subvehamitis, non autem ut in illis Adminiculis haercatis: Ita enim fieret, ut non vestra essent illa, sed illprum potius essetis:* Beza in *Annot ad 1 Cor. 3:22.*

(1) God's treasure—and that's Christ the Mediator; Christ is God's.

(2) Christ's treasure—and that's his saints, his mystical body; you are Christ's.

(3) The saints' treasure in Christ—and that's all things; all things are yours.

These three are well explicated by *oecumen* saying: all things are yours as your benefits and gifts. You are Christ's as his creatures and workmanship. Christ is God's as his generation and Son.[51]

Now, the saints' treasure in and by Christ *is*,

(1) More generally propounded—all things are yours, and this, after sundry instances is again reduplicated and repeated for the greater emphasis.

(2) More particularly expounded and illustrated by an induction of particular instance, that is,

a. All the ministers and teachers are yours. Therefore, glory in none.

b. The world is yours. Therefore, do not serve it, but make it serve you.

c. Life is yours. Therefore, use it aright; live to the Lord.

d. Death is yours. Therefore, do not dread it, but prepare for it and die to the Lord.

---

[51] *Oecum in Comment. ad 1 Cor. 3.*

e. Things present are yours. For your benefit and consolation in this world.

f. Things to come are yours also. For your bliss and glorification in the world to come.

Or, here's an excellent scale or series of subordinate ends; and of things referred to these their ends respectively, where they have more immediate tendency and subordination.

And these are especially three, *that is,*

(1) The saints and members of Christ (for to such he here wrote, 1 Cor. 1:2)—they are the first and lowest end here mentioned. To them, as to their immediate end, are subordinated, the ministers, the world, life, death, things present, things to come, and *all* things. All these are made contributory and subservient to the saints, for their benefits, edification, and eternal salvation, (1 Cor. 3:21-22).

(2) Christ—he (as Mediator) is the second end and superior to the former. To him, his service and glory, as to their immediate end, all the saints and whole body of Christ, is and ought to be subordinate, (1 Cor. 3:23).

(3) God—he is the third and supreme end. To him as to his immediate end, Jesus Christ the Mediator is subordinate that God in all things may be glorified, (1 Cor. 3:23).

3. Propositions, here resulting, are many. Especially these, *that is,*

(1) Christ the Mediator is God's, and God is his end.

(2) The saints are Christ's, and Christ is their end.

(3) All things are the saints, and the saints are their end. And under this third more particularly are comprised these propositions, *that is,*

a. They who are Christ's have all his ministers theirs.

b. They who are Christ's have the whole world theirs.

c. They who are Christ's have life and death theirs.

d. They who are Christ's have things present and things to come theirs.

e. They who are Christ's have all things theirs.

So, you may see, here's an ample field of matter discovered. To treat of all these at this time is neither possible, nor pertinent to this solemnity. From among all the rest, I shall single out only one doctrinal proposition, as being more peculiarly apposite to the present occasion, *that is,*

DOCTRINE: *They that are Christ's have life theirs and death theirs.*

They that are Christ's are his in deed and in truth. Not only in name, but also in nature; being new creatures, (2 Cor. 5:17), and partaking the divine nature, the true image of God, (2 Peter 1:4; Eph. 4:24 with Col. 3:10). Not only in form outwardly by a mere visible profession, but also in power inwardly by a holy constitution attended with an answerable conversations, (Matt. 25:3-4; 2 Tim. 3:5; Rom. 2:28-29; 1 John 2:6).

These have life theirs and death theirs. Life, their day to labor in; death, their night to rest and sleep in. Life, their race to run in; death, their goal to obtain the prize in. Life, their sea to fail in; death, their haven to land in. Life, their Egyptian pilgrimage under the many oppressions of their enemies; death, their Red Sea, delivering them, but overwhelming all their oppressors. Life, their long wilderness progress towards the heavenly Canaan; death, their roaring Jordan to be passed through at their entrances into the heavenly country flowing with milk and honey. Life, their time of conflict and tribulation; death, their time of conquest and coronation. Life, their holy time of preparation for the Lord; death, their happy time of transmigration to the Lord.

But waving generalities, let's come to a more particular illustration of this proposition. And here we shall inquire: (1) What's here *meant* by life and death? (2) How life is theirs who are Christ's? (3) How death is theirs, as well as life? (4) When it comes to pass, that life and death are so theirs, who themselves are Christ's?

What's here meant by life and death?

Chrysostom seems by these to understand the life and death of their teachers, that as they live, so they undergo perils and death itself for the body of Christ his church. And further, he thinks it may be said as to death: [θάνατος (1 Cor. 3:21).]. That is today that Adam's death was for us that we may be corrected (or nurtured). Christ's death that we may be saved. But (*pace tanti viri*, by the good leave of so grave an author) life and death here are not intended either of their teachers, or of Adam, or of Christ, but of the life and death of the saints and members of Christ, as the flow of the words evidently shows. Besides, that phrase—*all things are yours, whether Paul, or Apollo, or Cephas*—sufficiently comprehends all things in their ministers; office, gifts, graces, life, death, *etc.*, here asserted to be theirs. And as for the death of Adam, or of Christ; nor text, nor context afford the least color for any such interpretation. But they that are Christ's, life is theirs and death theirs. The life which themselves shall here live, and the death which themselves shall die; both are theirs for their great good and manifold advantage.[52]

But note, life and death are of three sorts, that is, natural, corporal, or temporal, (I list not to be too critical upon terms). Style it which you will, so you rightly understand the thing: spiritual, eternal. Now here we are not to understand life and death, spiritual or eternal; but only life and death natural, corporal, or temporal. (Rom. 14:7-9; Eph. 2:1-5; Matt. 25:46).

---

[52] John Chrysostom *in 1 Cor. 3. Hom. 10. p 99 D.E. Chrysostom ibid.*

Life, natural or temporal, is one of our dearest temporal enjoyments in this present world. All that a man has will he give for it, (Job 2:4). It consists generally in the vital union of matter and form, of body and soul. Life (said one) is the soul's abode in the body. But here three things must be distinguished, that is, *principium vivendi; esse viventis operationes vitae.* (1) *Principium vivendi*, the principle of living. And that's the form or soul: vegetative in plants, sensitive in brutes, intellective or rational in man. (2) *Esse viventis*—the being of the living which is properly such a nature in the living creature, while the principle of natural life is in it as whereby it is disposed to exert and exercise acts of life. (3) *Operationes vitae*—the operations or acts of life. Properly and formally these are not life, but the effects, fruits, and evidences of life. These acts of life may be reduced to motion, "In him we live, and move," (Acts 17:28). Every creature that lives, moves, and as the motion in any creatures is more or less perfect; so the life of them is more or less perfect. So, living plants do move by nourishing themselves, growing, fruit-bearing, and breeding their like, In this way, living brutes move by all the said motions of plants and over and above them; by outward senses: seeing, hearing, *etc.*, by inward senses. The common sense fantasy and memory, and by locomotion, or moving from place to place. So, living man moves by all the motions of both plants and brutes; and above them all by understanding, conscience, and will. The motion of brutes is more perfect than that of plants, and consequently, the life of brutes is more perfect than the life of plants. But the motion of man is more perfect than the motion of plants or brutes; and therefore, man's natural life is incomparably more perfect, noble, and excellent than theirs.[53]

Death, natural or temporal, is the privation of life natural through the separation of the matter from the form, of the body from the soul. In the death of plants or brutes, the form of soul is so severed that it's destroyed with the body as it goes downward. But in the death of man, his soul is so separated that it separately subsists without the body and goes upwards, and it returns to God to be immediately disposed by him to eternal weal or woe, (Eccl. 12:7, 3:21; 1 Kings 17:21-22; Heb. 9:27, 12:23; Luke 23:43, 16:22-23; 1 Peter 3:19).

Now, those that are Christ's have life and death, natural, corporal, or temporal, theirs: theirs peculiarly, theirs advantageously, beneficially, and salutiferously.

II. How is life *theirs* who are Christ's?

---

[53] *Vita est mansio animae in corpore. Vivere, viventibus est esse.*

Resolved: They who are Christ's have natural life theirs in a far and more excellent sort than any Christless person has it, *that is,*

1. As a token of God's paternal favor—they that are Christ's have life, not only from God as a common Creator, but also from God as a peculiar tender Father in Christ. "For your heavenly Father knoweth that ye have need of all these things," (Matt. 6:32). "Our Father which art in heaven...Give us this day our daily bread," (Matt. 6:9, 11). Again, "He that spared not his own Son, but delivered him up for us all, how shall he not with him also freely give us all things?" (Rom. 8:32). They have life, not only with God's leave and permission, but also with God's love and approbation; not only by God's general providence and common donation, but also by God's special providence and peculiar dispensation. Now the *affectus amantis,* the affection of the lover, is that which highly commends the *munera dantis,* the gifts of the giver; and is more than the gifts themselves. This makes the present life of the saints doubly sweet.

II. As an additional mercy in and with Jesus Christ—Jesus Christ is the gift of God, [δωρεὰν τοῦ θεοῦ], the primary, transcendent, and super-eminent gift of gifts, (John 4:10, 3:16). All others are but additional, accessory, and appurtenance attending upon him. Accessories follow the principals. Christ is the grand mercy, the mercy of mercies. Until we have obtained him, we have in effect obtained *no mercy*, (1 Peter 2:10). But to whom God gives Christ, to them he gives freely both life and all things with Christ, (Rom. 8:32, Matt. 6:33). He is the inheritance; these are but the appurtenances. He is the fountain; these but the streams then flowing. To them that are Christ's, he brings all blessings in his arms. As Christ's blood flows freely to them; so life and all things come sweetly swimming to them in the blood of a Savior.[54]

III. As a fruit of God's precious promises—Christless men have life and all their enjoyments only by common providence; but they that are Christ's have and hold life and all things by covenant and promise. Godliness has the promise of the life that now is and of that which is to come, (1 Tim. 4:8). Again, the promise is, "seek ye first the kingdom of God, and his righteousness, and all these things shall be added unto you," (Matt. 6:33). They that are Christ's are, "children of the Covenant with God made with Abraham," (Acts 3:25). They that are Christ's are, "Abraham's seed and heirs according to the promise," (Gal. 3:28-29, 4:28), while all others are, "strangers from the Covenant of Promise," (Eph. 2:12). Now to hold this by promise is both a sure and sweet tenure. For, "God that promised cannot lie," (Titus 1:2). Yes, God's

---

[54] *Christus ipse est Donum Dei primatium et maxime principale: caetera omnia sunt tantum modo accessoria. Accessorium autem sequitur principaie. S.S.*

promise and oath are those two immutable things wherever it is impossible for God to lie and this ministers to us as a strong consolation, (Heb. 6:18). And, "all the promises of God in Christ are yea, and in him amen," (2 Cor. 1:20). O! what an advantage is this to them that are Christ's, that hold life and all of God in Christ by promise! As Augustine notes: God has made himself their debtor, not by receiving from them, but by promising to them. They may by faith confidently rest and rely upon his promise. They may by prayer in all wants and changes plead God's promise and sue him (as it were) upon his own covenant and bond. He will not, "He cannot *deny himself*," (2 Tim. 13).[55]

IV. He is to them as a happy season divinely blessed and sanctified to all that are Christ's, for their salvifical furtherance in spirituals and eternals, (Titus 4:15, 2 Cor. 6:2). Others have life, but not in such a sort as sanctified. They (as one said) not so much live, as are *in life*. Life to them is as the quails were to Israel, a curse rather than a blessing. Or, as the pearl is to the muscle or oyster or the precious stone to the serpents head, they are diseases, rather than their perfection. Hereafter the wicked shall say that it had been good for them

---

[55] 2 Peter 1:4 with 1 Tim. 4:8; Matt. 6:33; *Fidelis Deus qui se nostrum debitorem fecit: non aliquid a nobis accipeiendo, sed tanta nobis pormittendo. Parum arat promissin; oriam scriptoli teneri volmir, veluti faciens nobiscum chirographum promissorum suorum.* Augustine *Enarrat in Psalm 109 as init. Tom. 8. Non tam vivunt, quam in vita sunt. Sen.*

that they had never lived, that they had never been born, (Matt. 26:24). Or that as soon as they were born alive, they had instantly died. But to the godly, life and all things are sweetly sanctified, the curse is removed; the free, lawful, comfortable, and beneficial use is restored, (1 Tim. 4:4-5; Gal. 3:9-14). To the pure all things are pure, but to them that are defiled and unbelieving, is nothing pure; but even their mind and conscience is defiled.[56]

Now, to them that are Christ's, this temporal life here on earth is so sanctified and blessed, as (in reference to the spirituals and eternals) *to be,*

1. Their holy seed time—their seed time of grace and glory. In this life they have their season to time accepted, their day of salvation. In this life, their eternal life is begun, (John 3:36, 17:3). The foundation stones of their salvation are laid—their eyes are opened, and they are turned from darkness to light, and from the power of Satan, to God, that they may receive forgiveness of sins, and inheritance among them that are sanctified through faith that is in Christ, (Acts 26:18). As they were, before the foundation of the world was laid, eternally predestinated, (Rom. 8:29-30).[57]

2. Their spiritual trading time—in this life, they that are Christ's have an excellent opportunity of driving their

---

[56] Psalm 78:27-32, 106:14-15; Titus 1:15.
[57] 2 Cor. 6:2.

spiritual trade to their eternal advantage. Their Lord and Master Jesus Christ has gone into a far country to receive a kingdom and to return. And he has committed a stock of talents, of graces, gifts, endowments, opportunities, *etc.*, to every one of his servants during his absence, that they may wind and turn them, employ and improve them in their spiritual trade, for their master's benefit. To some five, to some two, to some one talent; of all which he will require an exact account at his return; and will according to their works remunerate them respectively, (Matt. 25:14-31). In this life they as wise merchants have the happy season of trafficking for spiritual pearls and treasures of greatest price, (Matt. 13:44-46). Now, they, "buy of Christ gold tried in the fire, that they may be rich and eye-salve that they may see, and white raiment that they may be clothed, and that the shame of their nakedness do not appear," (Rev. 3:18). The gold of Christ's pure doctrine, or of unfeigned faith, both of them more pure and precious than gold tried in the fire; the eye-salve of saving illumination and the white raiment of Christ's righteousness. Of all these spiritual commodities, Christ alone has the monopoly. Therefore, of him alone they buy them, and of him they have them without money and without price, (Isa. 55:1-3).[58]

---

[58] *Christus est ille, qui merces salutis caelitis venalts nobis promit et offert in Evangelio,*

3. Their striving time—in this life, they that are Christ's have a seasonable opportunity: (1) Of striving to "enter in at the straight gate, leading to life, which few do find," (Luke 13:24); (2) of "contending earnestly for the faith once delivered to the saints," (Jude 3); (3) Of striving as wrestlers against all spiritual antagonists, (Eph. 6:12), as soldiers to fight the good fight of faith against all spiritual enemies, the world, flesh, and the devil, (2 Tim. 4:7; Eph. 6:11-12), as racers to run with patience the race that is set before them; yes, so to run, as to obtain the crown, (Heb. 12:1; 1 Cor. 9:24). Forgetting those things that are behind, they press towards the mark for the prize of the high calling of God in Christ Jesus, (Phil. 3:13-14).

4. Their trying time—in this life, they that are Christ's have many trials; but all for their good. They are tried by temptation—to discover the good that's in them—as Abraham was tried, (Gen. 21:1; Heb. 11:27). They are tried by tribulations to refine and purge away the evil that is in them, (Zech. 13:9; Isa. 27:9). They are tried by persecutions and fiery trials that they may be partakers of Christ's sufferings, and so may have the greater joy and crown at Christ's appearing, (1 Peter 4:12-13; Rev. 2:10). The wheat will not be clean without

---

non precio vel mei itis parandas, sed precibus et fide gratis a Deo accipiendas. Hoc est Christi, extra quod nulla est salus. Falluntur ergo qui a Sanctus salutem petunt. Impostor est Papa, qui indulgentias et Gaelum auro vendit. D.Pa.eus in Comment. ad Rev. 3:18.

the fan; the gold will not be pure without the fire and fining pot; the pomander smells the better for rubbing; the spice becomes the more fragrant by bruising; and the strings of the musical instrument, when stricken, makes the sweetest melody. So, are they that are Christ's, exceedingly bettered by all variety of their temptations and tribulations, (Heb. 12:6-10; Rom. 5:4-5, 8:28; 2 Cor. 4:17). Yes, this life is the saints' most happy season for searching and trying their own hearts and ways so that they may make their calling and election sure and may know that Christ is in them and that they are not reprobates, (2 Peter 1:10; 2 Cor. 13:5).

5. Their growing time—in this life they that are Christ's have an excellent opportunity of spiritual growth in grace and in the knowledge of Jesus Christ our Lord, (2 Peter 3:18), as did those eminent Babylonians of whom Paul testified, "Your faith groweth exceedingly (the Greek means over-grown, *abundantly* grown) and the charity of every one of you all towards each other aboundeth," (2 Thess. 1:3). And no wonder that in this life, they that are Christ's so grow and shoot forth. For, it is now that they have the ministers of Christ of all sorts planting and watering them, (1 Cor. 3:6). Now they have the Gospel ordinances moistening and seeding them, (1 Peter 2:2). And, which is most of all, now they have the enlivening sunshine of God's favors from heaven influencing them and causing them to increase, (1 Cor. 3:6-7).

And all this makes them exceedingly grow and flourish in all spirituals day by day.

6. Their fruit bearing time—in this life they that are Christ's have the very season of spiritual fruitfulness. Now they are as trees planted by the rivers of waters, giving forth their fruit in due season, (Psalm 1:3). Now the north wind awakes and the south comes and blows upon their garden that the spices of it may flow out, that Christ their beloved may come into his garden and eat his pleasant fruits, (Song of Solomon 4:16); that is, the fruits of holiness, righteousness, sobriety; of faith, love, meekness, humility, *etc.* even all the precious fruits of the Spirit together with all those pious exercises of hearing, praying, meditating, almsgiving, and all good-works, (Rom. 6:22; Eph. 5:9; Gal. 5:22-23). Now they are an orchard of pomegranates with pleasant fruits, camphor with spikenard, spikenard and saffron, calamus and cinnamon, with all the trees of frankincense, myrrh, and aloes with all the chief spices, (Song of Solomon 4:13-14). Now, now in this life (O Christians!) is all your fruit-bearing time. This is your golden season for believing, repenting, mortifying of sin, vivifying of grace, *etc.*, there's no place for any such things in the grave. This grace cannot praise God, death cannot celebrate him; they that go down into the pit, cannot hope for his truth. The living, the living shall praise him. The father to the children shall make know his truth, (Isa. 38:16-19).

Therefore, now let the counsel of Solomon sink deep into every true Christian's heart. "Whatsoever thine hand findeth to do, do it with all thy might; for there is no work, nor device, nor knowledge, nor wisdom in the grave whither thou goest," (Eccl. 9:10).

7. Finally, their hoarding time for eternity—in this life they that are Christ's "lay up for themselves treasures in heaven where neither moth nor rust doth corrupt, nor thieves break through and steal," (Matt. 6:20). Now they treasure up gifts, graces, prayers, tears, promises, experiences, evidences for heaven, *etc.* Now they may be rich in good-works, ready to distribute, willing to communicate; laying up in store for themselves (bags that do not wax old), and a good foundation against the time to come that they may lay hold on eternal life, (1 Tim. 6:19). Now they may make themselves friends with the mammon of unrighteousness, that when they fail, they may be received into everlasting habitation, (Luke 16:9). Now they may meditate of their mortality and prepare for their immortality. Now they may ponder upon their first, middle, and last things (as Bernard ranks them); those bring shame, those grief, and these fear. They may think this where they are and groan wherever they go and tremble. They may remember

their latter end that they may not easily do amiss. Thus, life is theirs.[59]

How is death theirs that are Christ's?

Resolve: As I have discovered the bright day of life to be theirs, so now I shall show how the dark night of death is theirs also. It's appointed to all men, godly and wicked, once to die, (Heb. 9:27). But O! what a vast disparity is there between the godly that are Christ's and the wicked that are Christless in death!

To the wicked belong the terrors of death, (Heb. 2:15), that king of terrors, as Bildad calls it, (Job 18:14), that most terrible of terribles as the heathen described it. The enmity of death, (1 Cor. 15:25-26), the sting and venom of death, (1 Cor. 15:56), the curse and bitterness, gall and wormwood of death, (Ga. 3:10), the woeful followers of death, that is, the judgment of condemnation, (Heb. 9:27; John 5:29), and everlasting torments in hell, (Matt. 25:41-46, Luke 16:23).

But for those that are Christ's, all this evil and mischief of death is sweetly removed away by Christ. (1) They do not fear death, but can desire it and groan after it. Having a desire to depart and to be with Christ, which is much better (Heb.

---

[59] *Fili, memorare novissima tua, et in aeternaum non peccibus. Revole primordia; Attende Media; Memorare Novissima uta. Haec pudorem adducunt, ista dolorem ingerunt, illa metum incatiunt. Cogita unde veneris, et erubesce; Ubi sis, et ingemisce; Qovadas, et contremisce.* D. Bernard *Serm. de Primardiis et Novissimus nostris, ad init* p. 376. Anwarp, 1616.

2:14-15; Phil. 1:23). "Lord, now lettest thou thy servant depart in peace, according to thy Word," (Luke 2:29). For in this we groan earnestly, desiring to be clothed upon with our house which is from heaven, (2 Cor. 5:2-4). (2) Of an enemy, death is become their friend; of loss, their gain, (Phil. 1:21; 2 Cor. 5:1). (3) Of an hornet, death is become a drone. The sting of death is plucked out by Christ, who have given them the victory, (1 Cor. 15:54-57). (4) The curse of death is turned into a blessing; "Blessed are the dead which die in the Lord, from henceforth, yea, saith the Spirit, that they may rest from their labors, and their works do follow them," (Rev. 14:13). (5) And the consequences of death are to them most comfortable, that is, the judgment of absolution, (Heb. 9:37 with Matt. 25:34), and eternal life in heaven, (Matt. 9:27; Luke 16:22). So, to them that are his, Jesus Christ brings light out of darkness, good out of evil, life out of death. He turns this venomous viper, death, into a sovereign golden syrup. Death is as Sampson's roaring lion, slain by Christ our true Sampson; out of whose carcass he gave his members the sweetest honeycombs of spiritual advantages.[60]

More particularly, let them that are Christ's know *that*,

1. Death is their sweet sleep in Jesus. It's often described, *their sleep*, (as John 11:11-13; Acts 13:36; 1 Cor. 15:51,

---

[60] *Ecce favus mellis stillat de ventae Leonis.* S.S.

11:30). And sometimes, *their sleep in Jesus,* as "them also which sleep in Jesus, will God bring with him," (1 Thess. 4:14). "Then they also which are fallen asleep in Christ are perished," (1 Cor. 15:18). The grave is their bed—"they shall rest in their beds," (Isa. 57:2). It is said of godly King Asa, "they buried him and laid him in the bed, which was filled with sweet odors and diverse kinds of spices prepared by the apothecaries art," (2 Chron. 16:14). But the saints' last bed, the grave, is perfumed with better sweets than spices and odors, even with the burial of Christ's own blessed body, (Matt. 27:59-60). In these beds they rest from all their labors of sin and sorrow, (Rev. 14:13). Here they sweetly sleep as in the bosom of Christ, to whom even their dead dust remains still mystically united; and therefore, is of precious account with him. And out of this last sleep they shall again awake at Christ's glorious appearing, (Dan. 12:2; 1 Cor. 15:23, 51-52; 1 Thess. 4:14-16).

2. Death is their alteration not their abolition; their change, not their confusion. Thus, Job accounted it, "All the days of my appointed time will I wait, till my change come," (Job 14:14). And of all men in the world, they that are Christ's do at death make a happy change; they change earth for heaven—an earthly, clay tabernacle for celestial mansions in the heavenly Father's house, (2 Cor. 5:1; Job 14:2), rags of morality for robes of immortality, (2 Cor. 5:4; 1 Cor. 5:4; 1 Cor. 15:53), and society of saints imperfect for the company of

blessed angels and of the spirits of the just men made perfect, (Heb. 12:23). As Jerome said of Nepotianus, "He did not so much die as remove, not so much leave his friends as change them. In all respects they change every way for the better.[61]

3. Death is their departure, not their destruction—their dissolution, not their reversion; "Having a desire to depart," (Phil. 1:23). Their loosing from this earthly shore to set sail for heaven, good old Simeon said, "Lord, now loosest thou thy servant, or lettest thou loose thy servant," (Luke 2:29). They depart from this Egypt and wilderness to that Canaan; from this earthly to that better and heavenly country, from this decaying city below to that continuing city above, (Heb. 13:14); from visibles to invisibles; from transitory and finite creatures; to God the Creator and Jesus Christ the Redeemer blessed forever, amen, (John 20:17; Phil. 1:23; 1 Thess. 4:17; Rom. 9:5).

4. Death is their gain, not their loss—so the apostle judged it would be to him, "For, to me to live is Christ and to die is gain," (Phil. 1:21). What gain? They that are Christ's when they die, lose their dearest natural lives, and there, their earthly relations and acquaintance, their friends, house, lands, livings, honors, riches, pleasures, even all these temporal enjoyments. True. But what are all these? Painted shadows,

---

[61] *Intelligeres illum, non emori, sed emigrare; et mutare amicos, non reliquere, Heir. in Epit. Nepot. tom. I. p. 25. A. Basil 1553.*

vanishing bubbles, magnified *nothings*. They gain by dying, other manner of treasures, as perfection of grace, possession of glory, the inheritance of heaven, the society of saints and angels, the immediate fruition of Christ and beatific vision of God forever face to face, (Heb. 12:23; John 17:24; 1 Thess. 4:17; Matt. 5:8; 1 John 3:2). All their losses are nothing to these gains.

    5. Death is their Red Sea affording them an eternal escape from all evils and dangers, but swallowing up all their enemies forevermore. Then they cease from sin, which shall no more defile them, (Rom. 6:7). Then they rest from their labors, which shall no more weary them, (Rev. 24:13). Then God shall wipe away all tears from their eyes and there shall be to them no more death, pain, sorrow, nor crying, (Rev. 21:4). Then no fiery darts of diabolical temptations shall evermore reach them. Then the wicked shall cease from troubling and the weary shall be at rest, (Job 3:17).

    6. Death is their body's seed-time, for a hopeful crop at the harvest of the resurrection. Tertullian said excellently, "The confidence of Christians is the resurrection of the dead." But the apostle Paul most sweetly, that which you sow is not quickened except it die. And that which you sow, you sow not that body which shall be, but bare grain, it may chance of wheat, or of some other grain; but God gives it a body as it has pleased him and to every seed his own body—so also is the

resurrection of the dead; it is sown in corruption, it is raised in incorruption; it is sown in dishonor, it is raised in glory; it is sown in weakness, it is raised in power; it is sown in natural body, it is raised a spiritual, (1 Cor. 15:36-44)—a wet and sad seed-time, but a joyful and happy harvest.[62]

7. Finally, death is their soul's birthday of eternal life. As it is the omega to all their miseries in the world present, so is the alpha to all their felicities in that world to come. Then the voice from heaven said to them, "Come up hither," (Rev. 11:12). O! the day of their dissolution will be to them a great, a happy, a glorious day indeed! Their redemption from all their sin and sorrow, (Rom. 6:7; Rev. 4:13); their translation into the better country, that is the heavenly; their entrance into their Master's joy, (Matt. 25:21-23). The daybreak of their endless Sabbath, (Heb. 4:9, Rev. 14:13); the inchoation of their eternal jubilee; their heavenly coronation day with that far more exceeding and eternal weight of glory, (2 Tim. 4:7; 2 Cor. 4:17). Yes, their blessed marriage day with the Lamb, in whose immediately vision and fruition their ravishments shall be unutterable and their entrancements unspeakable, (John 17:24). The enjoyment of Christ in heaven is the very heaven of

---

[62] *Fiducia Christianorum, resurrection mortuarum. Tertul. lib. de Resur. carnis, cap. I.* p. 314. France 1597.

heaven. So, to them that are Christ's, out of death that great eater comes meat and out of strength comes sweetness.[63]

IV. When is it that in this way life and death become theirs that are Christ's?

Resolve: All this comes to pass,

1. From all ordering purpose and providence of God towards them that are Christ's, who love him and are the called according to his purpose. He makes all things, good and evil, prosperity and adversity, life and death, *etc.*, cooperate for good to them. All things, not only some things; all things, not division, but conjunction; not severally, but jointly, one with another, and all which the influence of divine benediction. As all the wheels in a watch work together to tell the hour; and as all the ingredients in a medicine work together to effect the cure. "We know that all things work together for good to them that love God, that are the called according to his purpose," (Rom. 8:28). The Lord makes every wind to blow them profit; everything do them good.

---

[63] *Ah! We want Christ himself; and I should refuse heaven, if Christ were not there. Take Christ away from heaven, and it's but a poor, unheartsome, dark, waste dwelling. Heaven without Christ should look like the direful land of death. Mansions are but as places of briars and thorns without Christ; therefore, I would have heaven for Christ and not Christ for heaven. Formal blessedness is created, but objective happiness is an uncreated Godhead, etc.* Samuel Rutherford in his *Christ Dying, etc.* Epistle to the Reader, p. 10-11.)

2. From Christ's meritorious purchase—among many other glorious achievements of Christ, there are three very observable in reference to our present purpose, *that is,*

(1) Christ has obtained, regained, and restored all good to him, which the first Adam had forfeited and lost, (Col. 1:20; Matt. 6:33; Rom. 8:32; Titus 1:15).

(2) Christ has removed all the evil from his, which the first Adam had procured, (Titus 2:14; Gal. 3:13-14; Heb. 2:14-15).

(3) Christ turns that evil to good to his, which is not totally removed. Their sin makes them so much the more see the need and worth of a Savior, (Rom. 7:23-25). Their afflictions become great spiritual advantages, (Rom. 5:3-5, Heb. 12:6-10; 2 Cor. 4:17). Yes, their death itself is rendered to them a glorious gain, (Phil. 1:21-23, 2 Cor. 5:1-4). One well observed—the Covenant of Grace made no death, but found it in the world. Christ made of an old enemy death, a new servant; it's now the king's ferry boat to carry the children over the water. And I may add, through Christ's merit, to them that are Christ's, death is but a dark entry into their heavenly mansions; a churlish porter ushering into the

glorious paradise; a fiery chariot and whirlwind conveying them speedily to heaven, (2 Kings 2:11).[64]

3. From the predominant and inviolable concatenation of the causes of their salvation. They that are Christ's are predestined, called, justified and in some measure glorified, (Rom. 8:29-30). Therefore, if God is in this way for them, what shall prevailingly be against them? He that spared not his own Son, but gave him up freely for them, how shall he not with him also freely give them all things? (Rom. 8:31-32). Shall not life be theirs, and death theirs, and all things theirs for good? This indissoluble chain of salvation cannot be broken, by life, death, or any things. Therefore, life, death, and all things must comply to it, contribute to it, be wholly and universally subordinate and every way subservient to the accomplishing of it.

In this way we see how life and death are theirs that are Christ's; and where this comes to pass.

Now we come to certain consequences and inferences here, by way of *application*.

Here, what privilege persons are true Christians, above all Christless wretches, both in life and death! Parallel them a

---

[64] See Samuel Rutherford in his treatment of the *Covenant etc.* p. 141 chap 8. p. 47. This work is published by Puritan Publications called, "The Covenant of Life Opened."

little according to former discoveries and see what the Lord Christ has done for his, more than for all others.

They that are Christ's: (1) Have life theirs, their holy seed-time, their spiritual trading-time, their striving-time after best enjoyments, their trying-time in their spirituals, their growing time in grace and knowledge, their fruit-bearing time in all good works, and their hoarding time for life eternal; and (2) Have death theirs also, their sweet sleep in Christ Jesus, their perfective alteration not their abolition, their happy departure not their destruction, their great gain not at all their loss, their Red Sea delivering them but drowning all their enemies, their bodies seed-time for the glorious harvest at the resurrection, and their soul's birthday of eternal bliss.

They that are Christless, on the contrary, are naked and destitute of all these advantages both by life and death. Nor life, nor death are theirs, for good, but for harm; not their advantages, but their disadvantages; not their sanctified mercies, but their mischiefs, *etc.* "To them that are defiled and unbelieving, is nothing pure; but even their mind and conscience is defiled," (Titus 1:15). To them that are Christless and ungodly: (1) Their life in this world, what is itself, but their sinful seed-time to the flesh? (Gal. 6:8). Their wretched working and trading time in iniquity? (Matt. 7:23, Luke 13:27; Psalm 6:8). Their striving time only after earthly enjoyments? (Matt. 6:31-32; 1 Tim. 6:9-10). Their trying time to detect and draw forth their vileness? (Exod. 3:19-20, 14:17; Job 12:4-6). Their declining time wherein they wax worse and worse? (2 Tim. 3:13). Their barren time in which they bring forth nothing but briars and thorns, fruits of Sodom and Gomorrah and all pernicious works of the flesh? (Hab. 6:8; Deut. 32:32-33; Gal. 5:19-21). And, their unhappy season in which after their hardness and impenitent heart, they treasure up to themselves wrath against the day of wrath and revelation of the righteous judgment of God? (Rom. 2:5). (2) And, their death from this world, what is itself than the rotting of their flesh and bones, "full of the sins of their youth, which shall lie down with them in the dust?" (Job 20:11). Their woeful change of painted felicities for real miseries? (Luke 16:19-23). Their wretched departure from their wicked bodies until both souls and bodies shall depart from Christ? (Luke 16:22-23; Matt. 25:41). Their utter loss of all enjoyments on earth and of all hopes in heaven? (Luke 12:20-21; Heb. 9:27; Eccl. 9:10). Their fatal Red Sea overwhelming them forever? (Luke 16:22-26). Their body's bondage in the cursed grade and their soul's enthrallment in the prison of hell until the day of the Lord's vengeance shall overtake them both at his second appearing? (1 Peter 3:19; Heb. 9:27).

O! then let everyone consider these things and *say*: How happy are all that are Christ's, both in life and death! How wretched are all that are Christless, both alive and dead!

2. Therefore, why would you not now study and strive to become Christ's indeed? This, this is the only way to be truly rich, to be eternally happy. If the world, life, death, things present, things to come, all things, and all this theirs in Christ are able to do it. He that has Christ, his and himself is Christ's may sweetly say: *Christus meus, et omnia*; Christ is mine and all's mine. Therefore, when others say, *Who will show us good?* Do you say, "Lord lift up the light of thy countenance upon me," (Psalm 4:6-7). Lord, give me Christ, and then I have all.

3. Therefore, what a shame is it for Christians to have the least irksome or undervaluing thought of Christianity? When corruption within rebels against the Spirit in us, temptation from without perplexes us, afflictions toss and tire us, persecutions puzzle us, and the prosperity of the wicked amaze and dazzle our apprehensions. How are we then distempered and discomposed! Then, we have cleansed our hearts in vain and washed our hands in innocence. Then, we bless the wicked whom God abhors and speak against the generation of God's children, as once the psalmist did, (Psalm 73). Then we loath our spiritual manna and (like Israel) run back in our hearts again to Egypt. O! let us enter into the sanctuary of God and then all our misdeeming thoughts shall be reformed. O! all you that are Christ's, consider this text and

check yourselves for these your impudent and ungrateful misapprehensions. Christ is yours and you are Christ's; therefore, in Christ, life and death are yours and all things yours, for your manifold advantage. O! bless the Lord, that ever you were savingly acquainted with and interested in Christ and Christianity. Christ turns all your darkness into light; makes all your gall and wormwood, honey; turns your poisons into medicines; makes both your life and death both profitable and pleasant, like the land of promise flowing with milk and honey. Christianity is the right philosopher's stone indeed; turns all it touches into spiritual gold. Say, O! say it with much rejoicing—we are Christians; therefore, we are happy, both living and dying. "Whether we live, we live unto the Lord; whether we die, we die unto the Lord. Whether therefore we live, or die, we are the Lord's," (Rom. 14:7-9).[65]

Therefore, why should they that are Christ's be either weary of life or afraid of death? Are not both theirs? And theirs for the best? What wise man is weary of his welfare or afraid of his advantages? Especially when both of them are of a spiritual and eternal concernment? It's happy for Christians that they may live a while on earth, to be prepared for life eternal. And it's happy again for them that they may die and

---

[65] *Christiani sumus; Beati sumus, tam morentes quam viventes. S.S.*

depart from earth that they may go to possess their life eternal, for which they are prepared.

Therefore, how silently, self-denyingly and contentedly should all that are Christ's submit to God's disposal of them in all conditions; yes, both in life and death! Why? Because life's theirs, death's theirs, all's theirs. Every wind blows them profit. All things cooperate to their good, (Rom. 8:28). Do not murmur then at any divine dispensations, but be silent—yes—contented—yes—thankful in all. Consider how the saints of old behaved themselves in all, even the worst conditions, as Job, (Job 1:20-21), Eli, (1 Sam. 3:18), David, (Psalm 39:9), Hezekiah, (Isa, 39:8), Paul, (Phil. 4:11-13), yes, Jesus Christ himself, (John 18:10-11, Matt. 26:39-44); you walk as Christ walked, (1 John 2:6), and follow the saints as they followed Christ, (1 Cor. 11:1).

Therefore, finally, how thankfully should we rejoice in the life, and how patiently—yes—comfortably should we bear the death of dearest friends and relations that were truly Christian!—whether father, mother, husband, wife, *etc.*

Are they alive? Life is their spiritual seed-time to sow in; their mart-time to trade in; their race-time to run it; their spring-time to grow in; their summer to bear fruit in; their autumn to treasure up in for eternity; and their winter to be tried in that they may be found more precious than gold.

Are they dead? Mourn *moderately*. Comfort yourselves with this, that even death is theirs also; their sweet sleep is Jesus; their blessed change; their happy departure; their great gain; their Red Sea to all their evils and enemies; their bodies seed-time for the eternal harvest; and their soul's birthday of everlasting bliss.

So, I am done with my text. And now I know you expect I should super-add something in reference to this worthy person deceased; of whom we were unworthy. Should I say nothing of him, I doubt I should offend you. Should I say Much! I should offend myself.

He was one of the most eminent members of this famous city; well-known to you all, but more intimately to some and particularly to me. And did I not verily believe that he was one of Christ's and that life and death were his (as has been now explained) I should draw a veil of silence over him and hold my peace. (An alderman of the city and had been mayor in Aug. 1651.)

Promiscuous funeral eulogies touching both good and bad deceased is both against my judgment and practice. For (1) by this such praises are often misplaced upon the unworthy. And (as one said) many are commended (on earth) where they are not; while they are tormented (in hell) where they are. (2) By this the wicked are encouraged and hardened in their wickedness that they should not depart from it; the godly grieved, whom the Lord would not have made sad; the ministry reproached and God dishonored.[66]

But when persons eminent for piety and goodness are commended, (1) not so much they, as the gifts and graces of God in them are commended. And such praises Christ himself approves of, (Matt. 26:13; Mark 14:9). (2) They are propounded as patterns for the imitation of the living. And we ought to walk in the way of good men, (Prov. 2:20), and to follow them, as they follow Christ, (1 Cor. 11:1). And, in what I have to say as to this, happy soul, I shall especially aim at these two ends, that is, to exalt the gifts and graces of the Lord in him, and to incite you to a Christian imitation of him. His life was such that it rather calls for our imitation than our commendation; as Augustine once spoke in a similar case.[67]

To this end (always excepting) his known frailties and infirmities, which yet were a burden to him and for which he was accustomed quickly to check himself, discovering his error. And which of all, even the best of God's people are wholly exempted from failings in this sinful life? Happy is he that has the fewest? I may justly borrow some of the exemplary characters of God's people of old in whose steps he

---

[66] Multi laudantur ubi non sunt, dum torquentur ubi sunt. Aug.
[67] Illa quidem anima in societatem fidelium recepta, laudes nec curat nec quaerit humanas; Tu imitationem, ego laudem; quanquam, sicut supta dixi, laudem ab hominibus jam non quaerat, imitationem vero tuam tantum quaerit, p. 637 C.D. et 638 D. et 639 A. Tom 2. Basil 1569.

walked, to set forth his virtues; wherein you shall do well to follow him. (Jam. 5:17; Jon. 4:1-9; *Nam vitiis nemo sine mascitur; Optimus ille est, qui minimis urgetur.* Horat.)

With Cornelius—he was a devout man that feared God and gave much alms and prayed to God always, (Acts 10:2).

With Nathaniel—he was an Israelite indeed, in whom was no guile, (John 1:47).

With David—he desired to behave himself wisely in a perfect way, to walk with his house with a perfect heart, (Psalm 101:2).

With Joshua—he resolved, whatever others did, that he and his house should serve the Lord, (Josh. 24:15).

With Job—he was upright, one that feared God and eschewed evil, (Job 1:1).

With Abraham—he commanded his children and household after him, to keep the way of the Lord, (Gen. 18:19).

With Noah—he was upright in his generation, and he walked with God, (Gen. 6:9).

With Enoch—he walked with God, and he was not, for God took him, (Gen. 5:22-24). And because God has taken him, the children and family left behind him are weeping; his friends and near relations are mourning; the ministry sighing, nor can I among the rest (as Jerome said in a similar case) dissemble my sorrow; the poor, refreshed often with his bounty, bewailing; and the generality of the city lamenting him. I verily believe that here are present this day many more mourners in heart than mourners in habit, for the loss of this eminent Christian. Yet, let us recollect ourselves and allay our grief a little; considering that our great loss is his greatest gain, (Phil. 1:21); that he is not *amistus*, but *praemissus*. He is not lost, but sent before us; we must, we do not know how soon, follow after. That the Lord in great mercy has lent us him so long. Therefore, Let us not so much mourn, that we have now lost such a one, as rejoice and bless God, that in this way long we have had such a one—as Jerome once comforted Heliordorus.[68]

And to speak of him a little with reference had to our present text; life was his and death is his.

1. Life was his. And how Christianly did he improve it!

As a magistrate and citizen, he desired to govern religiously and righteously; to suppress wickedness and profaneness and particularly Sabbath profanation, to encourage the good and deter the evil-doers. He knew well the state of this city's affairs and aimed much at its public wheel, without self-seeking. He was a man of a very public

---

[68] *Volvuntur per ora lachrymae et obfirmato animo non queo dolorem dissmulare quem patior.* Hieronym. in Epitaph Nept. p. 25 tom. I. *Nec doleas quod talem amiseris, sed gaudeas quod talem habueris.* Hieronym ad Heliodor. in Epit. Nepotian. p. 23 tom.I.

spirit, desiring the public good; and what evil he was not able publicly to redress, he was accustomed privately to lament.

As a merchant, he walked righteously and self-denyingly. The balances of deceit were not in his hands, nor a double-tongue in his mouth. He was as a father of merchants. He fetched his merchandise from far, but traded most for heaven. He was sometimes jealous and afraid (so abundantly God has blessed him), that these temporals flowed in too fast upon him; and like Luther, much desired the Lord that he would not put him off only with these earthly things.

As a household, he kept the way of the Lord in and with his household. By due sanctifying of the Lord's Day Sabbath; daily reading of the Holy Scriptures; daily presenting of his morning and evening incense of praise and prayer with his family to his God; and by frequent instructing of his household in the things of Christ.

As a Christian, he was sound in the faith in erroneous times; blameless and exemplary in his life in corrupt times; and an ornament to the Gospel and doctrine of God our Savior. His search and inquiries into the deep mysteries of religion were many and considerable; his devotion in secret was much. His humility in the midst of all his ample enjoyments was great and very observable. And his charity—yes—his bounteous liberality to the distressed poor and needy was well-known to be overflowing even to admiration.

So, he lived much in a short time (as Jerome said of Lucinius). And so, lived long by living well. For to live well is to live twice.[69]

2. Death now at last is his also—his sweet sleep in Jesus; his happy change; his blessed departure; his rich gain; his Red Sea to all his enemies; his body's seed-time for a better resurrection; and his soul's coronation day, marriage day, and entrance into his everlasting jubilee. After a short, but sharp conflict with a violent putrid fever, for about eleven days space, he put off this tabernacle to be clothed upon with his house from heaven. During the time of his sickness, as his thoughts, so his discourses, were much upon spirituals and his ejaculatory requests to the Lord for himself, his family, and for the public, were very fervent. This was one of his wishes in his extremities. O! that all the rich men in the city here beheld my condition and how little gold and wealth can help in such a day of distress! This was one of his ejaculations: *O Lord, do what you will with this mortal body, so you will show mercy and salvation to my poor immortal soul!* His last words were these or to this effect, but with much more amplifications, "Into thine hands, O Lord, I commend my soul and body," (Luke 23:46), both now and forevermore, through Jesus Christ mine only Savior and Redeemer, amen; I have done. And having said this,

---

[69] *Placita enim erat Deo anima illius; et in brevi spatio tempora multa complevit.* Hieronym in *Epitaph Lucinii ad Theodorm, p. 195. B. tom. I. Basil 1553.*

he sweetly fell asleep in Jesus, (Acts 7:59-60). In whose blessed bosom we leave him, until his second coming. (John 19:30)

Life was his; death is his; He is Christ's; and Christ is God's.

FINIS

παρακαλοῦντες ὑμᾶς καὶ παραμυθούμενοι καὶ μαρτυρόμενοι εἰς τὸ περιπατεῖν ὑμᾶς ἀξίως τοῦ θεοῦ τοῦ καλοῦντος ὑμᾶς εἰς τὴν ἑαυτοῦ βασιλείαν καὶ δόξαν. (1 Thess. 2:12).

Josephus Jackson Armiger and Aldermannus Civitatis de Bristol, Anborum 57 faeliciter obdormivit in Domino, Die Dominico January 5 circa horam 5 pomerid. Et perplurimis impense lugentibus, in Eccl. de Warborrough's in ead Civit. decenter inhumatus est, Januarii die 17 An. Dom. 1661.

www.ingramcontent.com/pod-product-compliance
Lightning Source LLC
Chambersburg PA
CBHW032042090426
42744CB00004B/96